Sister Sheila O'Keefe, C.S.C.

D0856068

Sister Sheila O'Keefe, C.S.C.

A
Holy Card
Prayer Book

A Compilation of Saints and Holy People

Text
Leaflet Missal Company Staff

Artist
Anna May McCallum

Nihil Obstat: Richard J. Schuler
Censor Deputatus

Imprimatur: ✝ John R. Roach, D.D.
Archbishop of St. Paul and Minneapolis

The Leaflet Missal Company

976 West Minnehaha Avenue Saint Paul, Minnesota 55104

Printed in U.S.A.

Dedication

We dedicate this book to St. Elizabeth Ann Seton, wife, mother and foundress, the first native-born American saint who opened the first American parochial school.

Table of Contents

Adoration of the Holy Eucharist

Adoration of the Holy Eucharist is the supreme honor and loving submission that is given to Jesus Christ, Whose Body, Blood, Soul and Divinity are truly present under the appearances of bread and wine. The reverence bestowed on Jesus, God the Son made man, honors God the Father and God the Holy Spirit, Who are the three Persons in one God. Eucharistic adoration was given a special prominence in 1916, when an angel of God appeared to three shepherd children in Fatima, Portugal, and told them of the importance of prayer. The third time he appeared to them he was holding a chalice of the Precious Blood and a Host above It, from which drops of Blood fell into the chalice. He taught them a prayer of reparation, and then together they prostrated before the Holy Eucharist with their foreheads touching the ground, and recited the reparation prayer, making amends for the sins committed against the love of God. God commands us to love Him above all things, and through the adoration of the Holy Eucharist, reparation is made for the lack of love of God, and it implores His mercy for sinners.

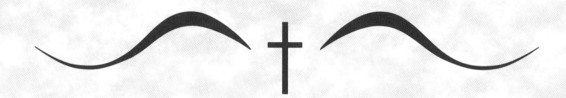

The Prayer of Reparation

O Most Holy Trinity, Father, Son and Holy Spirit, I adore Thee profoundly and I offer Thee the most Precious Body, Blood, Soul and Divinity of Jesus Christ, present in all the tabernacles of the world, in reparation for the outrages, sacrileges and indifference by which He is offended. By the infinite merits of the Sacred Heart of Jesus, and the Immaculate Heart of Mary, I beg the conversion of poor sinners. Amen.

Pardon Prayer

My God, I believe, I adore, I trust and I love Thee! I beg pardon for those who do not believe, do not adore, do not trust, and do not love Thee. Amen.

Blessed Sacrament Prayer

O Most Holy Trinity, I adore Thee! My God, my God, I love Thee in the Most Blessed Sacrament!

St. Agnes

Agnes was martyred during the reign of Diocletian around 304 at the age of thirteen. She was born in Rome, and at an early age decided to dedicate her virginity to God. Many young noblemen, attracted by her beauty and riches, sought her hand in marriage. But she told them that "Christ is my Spouse." They accused her of being a Christian, and brought her before a judge who threatened her with death by torture and fire unless she renounced her loyalty to Christ. Undaunted by his threats, the judge sent her to a prostitution house. She retained her purity and when brought again to the judge, he ordered her beheaded. St. Agnes is a virgin martyr of the early Church. Her name means "lamb." She is commemorated in the Canon of the Mass, and her feastday is Jan. 21.

St. Agnes, Patroness of Purity

O valiant maiden, most pure St. Agnes! By the burning love which inflamed thy heart and preserved thee from harm in the midst of the flames of passion and of the stake, with which the enemies of Jesus Christ sought to destroy thee; obtain for us from God that no unclean flame may set our hearts aglow but only that fire which Jesus Christ came to enkindle upon the earth, so that having spent a spotless life in the exercise of this beautiful virtue, we may merit to share in the glory which thou didst merit by the purity of thy heart and thy martyrdom. Amen.

St. Andrew Kim

Andrew Kim was born of a noble family in Korea in 1820. He was ordained to the priesthood in South China at Macao, and returned to Korea as its first native Catholic priest. His faith in God and love for the Christian people inspired him with a missionary zeal to witness for Christ despite the religious persecutions in his land. In 1846, just thirteen months after becoming a priest, he was put to death by the sword at the age of twenty-six. During the time of the persecutions, which lasted more than one hundred years, 10,000 were martyred in Korea. Andrew Kim was among the 103 martyrs that were canonized in Korea on May 6, 1984. Together they joyfully shed their blood for Christ and planted the seeds of the Catholic faith in Korea which caused the faith to blossom.

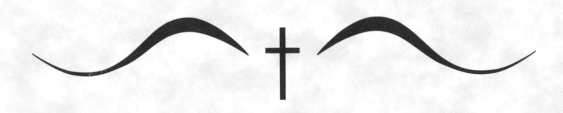

St. Andrew Kim

Lord our God, You give Your martyrs the grace to die for the love of Jesus Christ and the spread of His Gospel. May the prayers and life of Your holy martyr, Andrew Kim, give us the courage to endure our sufferings for love of You and to profess our faith in Jesus Christ and His Holy Catholic Church, that we may obtain the joy of everlasting life. Amen.

St. Anthony of Padua

Anthony was born in Lisbon, Portugal in 1195. He was educated in the Cathedral school of Lisbon, and at fifteen became a Canon Regular of St. Augustine. In 1212, he was permitted to join the Franciscans, taking the name of Anthony. His desire to be a martyr sent him on a mission to Africa. But illness forced him to return, and on the way back a storm blew his ship off-course toward Italy, which allowed him to visit St. Francis in Assisi. He was assigned to teach theology to his order, and later he began preaching to large crowds in the cities of Europe, converting many to the love of Christ. He was an untiring preacher, and very generous to the poor. He came to Padua, Italy in 1226, and his love for souls transformed the city through his superior preaching, converting many of the heretics. He died in Padua on June 13, 1231, was canonized the following year, and made a Doctor of the Church in 1946. He is known as the "Hammer of Heretics," and the "Wonder Worker," because he is credited with many miracles, one in which a mule prostrated before the Blessed Sacrament. He is frequently shown holding the Child Jesus, an event in his life observed by an eye-witness. He is the patron for finding lost articles.

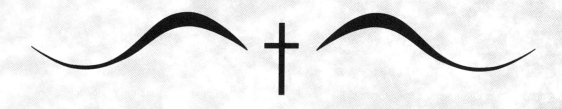

Prayer to St. Anthony

O gentle St. Anthony, by your holy and apostolic life, you led countless souls to the love of our Divine Lord. I implore you, obtain for me and my loved ones His guidance, you who have the power to lead straying sheep back to the fold of Christ, and to find articles that are lost. On earth your heart was filled with compassion for those in distress or sorrow. Please bring my request before the Child Jesus, Who loved to rest in your arms, and I believe that you will help me to remain always close to our Divine Lord. O miraculous Wonder Worker, in this hour of need obtain what I ask of you. Amen.

St. Benedict and St. Scholastica

Benedict was born around 480 in Nursia, Italy. He studied in Rome, but because of the city's decadence, he decided to become a hermit. For three years he lived in a cave, before becoming the spiritual leader of a community of monks. He fled after they resisted his religious rule and tried to poison him. He then established twelve monasteries of monks, and then founded a monastery at Monte Casino, which became the cornerstone of monastic life in the Church. His holiness of life attracted many followers, and he wrote a religious rule of life that stressed prudence, moderation, and work and prayer under the obedience of an abbot. Great reverence was given to the Divine Office. His sister, Scholastica, was the abbess of a nearby convent. Three days before she died, they met for a visit. After she prayed that the visit would linger, a sudden storm arose, and they spent the night in prayer and spiritual conversation. When she died, he saw her soul rise to heaven in the form of a dove. Shortly thereafter, he died after receiving Holy Communion on Mar. 21, 543. He was named patron of Europe and his name means "blessed."

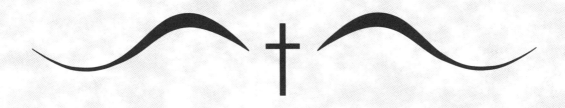

St. Benedict

God our Father, You made St. Benedict an outstanding guide to teach men how to live in Your service. Grant that by preferring Your love to everything else, we may walk in the way of Your commandments. We ask this through Christ our Lord. Amen.

St. Scholastica

O God, Who, to show us the way of innocence, didst cause the soul of Thy blessed virgin Scholastica to enter heaven in the form of a dove: grant us, by her merits and prayers, so to live in innocence, that we may deserve to attain to eternal joys. Through Christ our Lord. Amen.

St. Bernadette

Bernadette was born on Jan. 7, 1844, in Lourdes, France, and lived in poverty with her family and was uneducated. On Feb. 11, 1858, the Virgin Mary appeared to her in a grotto in Lourdes, and joined her in praying the Rosary. Our Lady had a Rosary on her arm, and wore a white dress with a blue sash and white veil, and had gold roses on each foot. During a series of visions, which lasted until July 16, she asked her to pray for sinners, and that a chapel be built at the grotto. Miraculous spring water began to flow after one of the apparitions. On Mar. 25, Our Lady revealed to her that "I am the Immaculate Conception." The Church approved the apparitions in 1862, and Bernadette joined the Sisters of Charity in Nevers in 1866. Lourdes became an international shrine for prayer and penance, where many were cured through the miraculous waters and the blessing with the Blessed Sacrament. The apparitions reaffirmed the dogma of the Immaculate Conception proclaimed and solemnly defined for an everlasting memorial by Pius IX on Dec. 8, 1854. Bernadette died on Apr. 16, 1879, and was canonized on Dec. 8, 1933, by Pope Pius XI.

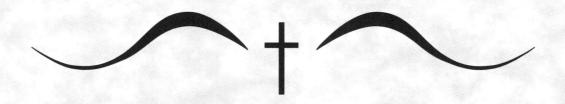

Prayer to Our Lady of Lourdes

O ever Immaculate Virgin, Mother of mercy, health of the sick, refuge of sinners, comfort of the afflicted, you know my wants, my troubles, my sufferings, deign to cast upon me a look of mercy. By appearing in the Grotto of Lourdes, you were pleased to make it a privileged sanctuary, whence you dispense your favors; and already many sufferers have obtained the cure of their infirmities, both spiritual and corporal. I come, therefore, with the most unbounded confidence to implore your maternal intercession. Obtain, O loving Mother, the granting of my requests. Through gratitude for favors, I will endeavor to imitate your virtues that I may one day share your glory. Amen.

St. Cecilia

Cecilia was born in Rome of a high class family and vowed to be a bride of Christ. Her family forced her to marry a pagan nobleman, but she converted him and he honored her virginity. He and his brother were later martyred, and Cecilia was arrested while burying their bodies. She refused to honor the Roman gods, and was sentenced to be suffocated in a hot-air bath in her home. She survived the ordeal, and the judge then ordered her beheaded. Her executioner failed in his attempt to behead her. For three days, she lay seriously wounded in her home, and then received Holy Communion before she died in 117. Cecilia is commemorated in the Canon of the Mass and is the patroness of sacred music.

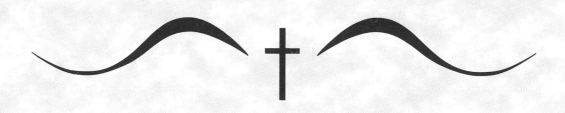

St. Cecilia

O God, by her chastity and her faith in Thy power, St. Cecilia was pleasing to Thee, and granted the crown of martyrdom. May we who celebrate her entry into heavenly glory draw nearer to Thee by her example. We ask this through Christ our Lord. Amen.

To St. Cecilia

O glorious St. Cecilia, virgin and martyr, you won the martyr's crown without renouncing your love for Jesus, the delight of your soul. We ask that you help us to be faithful in our love for Jesus, that, in the communion of the saints, we may praise Him twice in our song of rejoicing for the Blood that He shed which gave us the grace to accomplish His will on earth. Amen.

The Children of Fatima

Jacinta Marto, 7, and her brother Francisco, 9, along with their cousin Lucia dos Santos, age 10, were witnesses to six apparitions of the Virgin Mary in Fatima, Portugal from May 13 to October 13, 1917. Our Lady revealed to them that God wanted to establish devotion to the Immaculate Heart of Mary in the world, and she requested the consecration of Russia to Her Immaculate Heart. The children of Fatima were shown a vision of hell, and told to pray the Rosary daily for peace in the world, and to offer sacrifices for the conversion of sinners. Jacinta said, "how sorry I am for the souls who go to hell...I offer everything for sinners in reparation to the Immaculate Heart of Mary." Francisco said, "I love God so much. But He is very sad because of so many sins." He desired to "console Our Lord Who is so sad." His great joy was to have the "Hidden Jesus within my heart." Francisco died of influenza on Apr. 4, 1919, and Jacinta died of pleurisy on Feb. 20, 1920. Both were declared Venerable on May 13, 1990.

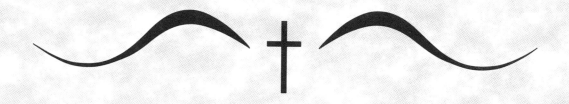

The Hail Mary

Hail Mary, full of grace, the Lord is with thee; blessed art thou among women, and blessed is the fruit of thy womb, Jesus. Holy Mary, Mother of God, pray for us sinners, now and at the hour of our death. Amen.

Fatima Prayer

O my Jesus, forgive us our sins, save us from the fire of hell. Lead all souls to heaven, especially those who are in most need of Thy mercy.

The Immaculate Heart

O Immaculate Heart of Mary, Queen of heaven and earth, and tender mother of men, I consecrate myself and all that I have to thee. Reign over us and teach us how to make the Heart of Jesus reign and triumph in us as It did in thee. May we be thine in joy and in sorrow, in life and in death. We promise to live a Christian life in imitation of thy virtues, to receive Holy Communion worthily, and to offer a daily Rosary, along with our sacrifices of reparation and penance. Amen.

The Crucifixion

The crucifixion of Jesus Christ on the cross on Calvary is the offering of His life to His heavenly Father to atone for the sins of mankind and to open the gates of heaven. Through the shedding of His Precious Blood, sins are forgiven, and man is reconciled to God and incorporated into His risen life through baptism, which is the death of sin, and the renunciation of Satan and the attractions of the world. The cross of Jesus is the divine power that triumphs over the wisdom of the world. It signifies the obedience of Jesus, His charity and self-sacrifice that His followers must imitate through Mary in the new life that He offers through the shedding of His Precious Blood. He is the Divine Lamb Who takes away the sins of the world, apart from Whom there is no salvation. We must approach His sacrifice on Calvary with the reverence and awe of the angels, and enter into it with love and gratitude when it is sacramentally re-enacted in the Holy Sacrifice of the Mass.

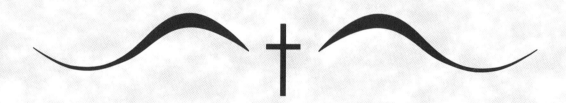

Prayer to Jesus Crucified

Behold, O kind and most sweet Jesus, I cast myself upon my knees in Thy sight, and with the most fervent desire of my soul, I pray and beseech Thee that Thou would impress upon my heart lively sentiments of faith, hope and charity with true contrition for my sins and firm purpose of amendment; while with deep affection and grief of soul I ponder within myself and mentally contemplate Thy five wounds, having before my eyes the words which David the prophet put on Thy lips concerning Thee: "They have pierced my hands and my feet, they have numbered all my bones."

Divine Mercy Prayer

Eternal Father, I offer You the Body and Blood, Soul and Divinity of Your dearly beloved Son, Our Lord Jesus Christ, in atonement for our sins and those of the whole world.

The Crucifixion and the Good Thief

God the Father sent His Son into the world to redeem mankind of its sins. Jesus, God the Son made man, was condemned to death for our sins and was nailed to a cross between two thieves. The Good Thief said, "Lord, remember me when you come into Your kingdom." Jesus said, "this day you will be with Me in Paradise." He recognized that Jesus was a Divine King and His suffering on the cross atoned for the sins of the world, unlike the bad thief who blasphemed, denying the fear of God and His just punishments. The Good Thief saw that the love of Jesus was insulted by the sins that nailed Him to the cross. As a sinner, he had taken what belonged to others, but through his repentance and belief in God's justice, Jesus promised him the possession of eternal life. His confession of faith made reparation for the sins committed against the holiness of God. The Good Thief shows that God is always ready to forgive repentant sinners, even on their deathbed, and that perseverance in the service of God merits the grace of a holy death.

With Me in Paradise

Dear Jesus! For love of me, You hung in agony upon the cross; and with such generosity You answered the faith of the Good Thief who, in Your suffering, acknowledges You to be the Son of God, that You assure him of paradise. Have pity, then, on all the faithful who are in their agony, and upon me. When I shall come to my death, breathe into my soul, by the merits of Your Most Precious Blood, faith so firm that will ward off the evil spirit, that I may enter into Your holy paradise. Amen.

For Perseverance

Lord our God, make me persevere in fulfilling Your will, and may I act at all times with patience, charity, joy and fidelity. May the virtues of modesty, continence and chastity adorn my soul, and, by Your grace, preserve me from all sin. Amen.

At the Hour of Death

O Jesus, I adore Thy dying breath and offer Thee my last moment that it be a perfect act of love for Thee. Amen.

St. Dymphna

Dymphna was born in the seventh century to a pagan chief of Celtic origin and a beautiful Christian mother. After her mother died, her father sent envoys throughout the land to find another wife of similar beauty who would marry the chief. He was persuaded that Dymphna was his only choice, but she declined, after consulting her spiritual director. The chief was determined to marry his daughter, but she fled to Belgium along with her spiritual director and two friends. They lived in seclusion and established their own chapel. But the chief found their place of hiding, and demanded that Dymphna return with him to be his wife. Both Dymphna and the priest explained to the chief that his proposal was immoral, but he ordered that the priest be beheaded, and then, enraged, he beheaded Dymphna, when she remained steadfast in her refusal to consent to an incestuous marriage. She was martyred around 620 at the age of fifteen. She is the patron of nervous and mental disorders.

St. Dymphna
Patroness of the Mentally Afflicted

Dearest St. Dymphna, gracious patroness of those suffering from afflictions of mind and body, I humbly implore your powerful intercession to Jesus through Mary, the Health of the Sick. Since you are filled with love and compassion for those who seek relief from their disorders, I beg you to show your love and compassion for me. The many miracles and cures which have been wrought by your prayers gives me great hope that you will help me in my present needs (*mention them*). O St. Dymphna, young martyr of purity, the fervent faith and devotion of the many souls you have helped by your charity, inspires me to entrust myself to your special care. I am confident of obtaining my urgent request, if be for the greater glory of God and the good of my soul. Help me to bear my sufferings with patience and resignation. May my prayer for the consolation and the cure of my illness be granted through your intercession. Amen.

St. Elizabeth Ann Seton

Elizabeth Ann Seton was born in New York City on Aug. 28, 1774, to a wealthy Episcopalian family. She was educated by her father, and was married in 1794. She raised five children, and did relief work for the poor. In 1803, her husband died while they were in Italy caring for his health. She returned to America, and due to her contact with the Catholic faith in Italy, she became a Catholic in 1805, despite the opposition of her family and friends. She accepted the offer to start a school for girls in Baltimore, and then founded the first American religious community, the Sisters of Charity of St. Joseph in 1809, which was later approved by Archbishop Carroll. She became the superior of the community, known as Mother Seton. Her community moved to Emmitsburg, Maryland and it grew to twenty communities. She had a great devotion to Mary, and said that Mary "loves our souls bought by the Blood of her Son." She died on Jan. 4, 1821, and was canonized the first native-born American saint on Sept. 14, 1975. The work of Mother Seton in religious education was influential in starting the Catholic school system in America.

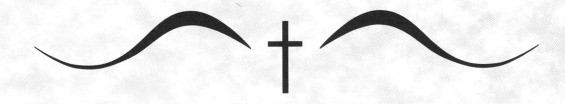

St. Elizabeth Ann Seton

Lord God, You blessed Elizabeth Ann Seton with gifts of grace as wife and mother, educator and foundress, so that she might spend her life in service to Your people. Through her example and prayers, may we learn to express our love for You in love for one another. We ask this through Christ our Lord. Amen.

Prayer of Mother Seton

I bow to You, my God, in cheerful hope, that confiding in Your infinite mercy, assisted by Your powerful grace, I shall soon arrive at that hour of unspeakable joy. But if it is Your will that the spirit shall yet contend with its dust, assist me so to conduct myself through this life as not to render it an enemy but a conductor to that happy state. Amen.

St. Francis

Francis was born in Assisi, Italy to a wealthy family around 1181. After hearing the Lord calling him to leave the world, he renounced his comfortable life, and embraced a life of complete poverty to the dismay of his father. He repaired the churches of Assisi, and then lived at a little chapel, the Portiuncula. His way of life attracted many followers, among them the wealthy, and with twelve of his disciples, he received permission from Pope Innocent III in 1210 to start a religious order of Franciscans. He assisted St. Clare in founding an order of Poor Clares. In 1216, Pope Innocent III granted him the Portiuncula Indulgence. Francis built a Christmas creche in 1223, which established a tradition in Christianity down to the present time. A year later, in a vision, he received the five wounds of Jesus. He died in Assisi on Oct. 3, 1226. Though he was never ordained, the gentleness, humility and simplicity of St. Francis and his love of God's creatures, has influenced many people from all walks of life. His love of God and man came from his devotion to the Passion of Christ.

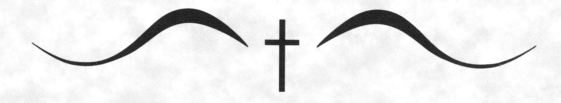

Prayer for Peace

Lord, make me an instrument of Your peace. Where there is hatred, let me sow love. Where there is injury, pardon; where there is doubt, faith; where there is despair, hope; where there is darkness, light, and where there is sadness, joy. O Divine Master, grant that I may not so much seek to be consoled, as to console; to be understood, as to understand; to be loved, as to love; for it is in giving that we receive; it is in pardoning that we are pardoned; and it is in dying that we are born to eternal life. Amen.

St. Gerard Majella

Gerard was born in Muro, Italy in 1726. He worked in the tailor trade, and eventually had a store of his own, before he joined the Redemptorists in 1748 as a lay brother. He was professed by St. Alphonsus, and performed his duties and tasks effectively. Because of his holiness, many miraculous events occurred due to his prayers. He had the supernatural gifts of bilocation, and especially prophecy, which allowed him to give counsel to religious communities. His service to the poor, hospitality to visitors and sanctity of life was a model of charity and obedience for the members of his community. He died on Oct. 15, 1755, at the age of twenty-nine, and was canonized in 1904 by Pope St. Pius X. He is patron of expectant mothers, because his prayers helped a woman who was about to give birth to a child.

St. Gerard, Patron of Motherhood

O glorious St. Gerard, powerful intercessor before God, I call upon you and seek your help. May you, who on earth always fulfilled God's will, help me also to do the holy will of God. Beseech the Master of Life, from Whom all paternity proceeds, to render me/her fruitful in offspring that I/she may raise up children to God in this life to be heirs of His kingdom in heaven for all eternity. O almighty God, Who, by the power of the Holy Spirit, prepared the body and soul of the Virgin Mary, the Mother of God, to be a worthy habitation of Your Son, listen to the prayer of Your child, who implores You through the intercession of St. Gerard. Protect me/her in the dangers of motherhood and safeguard against the evil spirit the tender fruit which You have vouchsafed to grant me/her in order that by Your saving hand the child may receive holy Baptism. May both I/she and my/her child, after living good Christian lives, attain everlasting happiness in heaven. Amen.

The Guardian Angel

Guardian angels are created pure spirits, messengers sent by God to guard and guide the faithful on the way to salvation. They are individual spirits and the faithful companions of baptized persons, leading them in the life of grace to love and follow Jesus, Who became man to destroy the works of the devil, and to adore Him in His real presence in the Holy Eucharist. The angel guardians are good angels, and each soul has a guardian angel, who contemplates and adores the mystery of one God in Three Divine Persons, and who protects him from spiritual adversity, and from the wickedness and snares of the devil and his fallen angels. The guardian angels serve and defend the majesty of God, and even protect individual countries. The Church has solemnly defined the existence of angels, and in 1670 Clement X established that Oct. 2 is the feast of the guardian angels for the entire Church.

The Guardian Angel

God Our Father, in a wonderful way You guide the work of angels and men. May those who serve You constantly in heaven keep our lives safe from all harm on earth. We ask this through Christ Our Lord. Amen.

The Holy Angels

God Our Father, in Your loving providence You send Your holy angels to watch over us. Hear our prayers, defend us always by their protection and let us share Your life with them forever in heaven. Amen.

Angel of God

Angel of God, my guardian dear, to whom God's love commits me here; ever this day be at my side, to light and guard, to rule and guide. Amen.

St. Helena

Helena was born in Asia around the year 250. She married a Roman officer in 270, and became the mother of Constantine the Great, the first Christian Emperor. After he miraculously defeated a formidable army and issued the Edict of Milan in 313, allowing Christians to freely practice their faith, Helena became a Christian and diligently practiced her faith. She was made empress by her son, and used her wealth to assist the poor, and to build churches in Rome and in the Holy Land. On a journey to Jerusalem in 326, she is credited with finding the True Cross on which Jesus died for the salvation of the world. She found it near Mount Calvary buried in a sepulcher with two others, and identified it when it was the only one when applied to a sick woman that cured her of her illness. After she brought a part of the True Cross to Rome and placed it in a church she built, St. Helena died in Rome in 328.

St. Helena

O Jesus! Through Thy burning love for us, Thou didst will to be nailed to the Cross and to shed Thy Precious Blood for the salvation of souls. In Thy divine plan, St. Helena found Thy triumphant Holy Cross and gave to the Church a priceless treasure. By her prayers, may we obtain the grace of eternal life won for us on Calvary through Thy life-giving Holy Cross. Amen.

The Holy Face

Devotion to the Holy Face of Jesus is the work of making reparation for the blasphemies committed against God's Divine Majesty. The devotion was made known through Sr. Mary of St. Peter, a Carmelite nun, who was born on Oct. 4, 1816, in Rennes, France. She joined the Carmelites in 1839 and was inspired with the spirit of sacrifice and zeal for the salvation of souls. She was devoted to the Hearts of Jesus and Mary, and to the Sacred Infancy of Jesus, desiring to be His "little donkey." In 1843, Our Lord gave her the Golden Arrow prayer of reparation, and revealed in 1845 that devotion to His Holy Face is the external object of adoration in the work of reparation for the blasphemies and outrages inflicted against His divinity, His Holy Name and His Church. By offering the Holy Face to the Father, God's anger is appeased, sinners are converted and the Divine image is restored in souls. Sr. Mary of St. Peter died on July 8, 1848, and Pope Leo XIII established the Archconfraternity of the Holy Face in 1885. Since then, the devotional life of St. Therese and the evidence of the Shroud of Turin have helped to revive the devotion to the Holy Face of Jesus.

The Golden Arrow

May the most holy, most sacred, most adorable, most incomprehensible and unutterable name of God be always praised, blessed, loved, adored and glorified in heaven, on earth and under the earth by all the creatures of God, and by the Sacred Heart of our Lord Jesus Christ in the most holy Sacrament of the altar. Amen.

Holy Face Prayer

Eternal Father, we offer You the Holy Face of Jesus, covered with blood, sweat, dust and spittle, in reparation for the crimes of communists, blasphemers, and for the profaners of the Holy Name and of the Holy Day of Sunday. Amen.

The Holy Family

The Holy Family is the spiritual union of Jesus, Mary and Joseph, brought about by the unbreakable union of the Virgin Mary and the Holy Spirit in the Incarnation of God the Son, and guarded by Joseph, the vicar of God the Father, in the home of Nazareth. Jesus, God the Son made man, is the Center of the Holy Family, and was subject to and honored the authority of Joseph and Mary. In His humanity, He grew in age and wisdom, but as God, He was concerned about His "Father's business." Mary, the Mother of God, is the lowly servant whose innocence and purity found favor with the Father, and who served the Child Jesus in faith and in charity during His childhood. Joseph, the just man and chaste spouse of Mary, set an example of obedience, patience, prudence and courage in his care for the needs of the Child Jesus. The Holy Family worked, prayed and worshipped together, and with Jesus, the source of grace in the home, they were a model of holiness for all families in their love of God and service to their neighbor. As the King and Center of all hearts, Jesus establishes the family of God on earth and in heaven in union with the Most Holy Trinity.

Jesus the Center of Our Family

O Lord Jesus, God of Love, You are the Center of our family. You humbled Yourself and came to live among us in Your home with Joseph and Mary. Take our family and let Your peace be with us. Guide us in our family decisions, in our needs and our worries, and in our work, play and study. Give us a strong faith and help us to do Your will. Amen.

Prayer to Jesus in the Holy Family

Lord Jesus Christ, Who, being made subject to Mary and Joseph, consecrated domestic life by Thine ineffable virtues; grant that we, with the assistance of both, may be taught by the example of Thy Holy Family and may attain to its everlasting fellowship. Who lives and reigns, world without end. Amen.

The Immaculate Heart of Mary

On the cross on Calvary, Jesus established devotion to the Immaculate Heart of Mary when He said, "Behold Thy Mother," and Our Lady reaffirmed it at Fatima, Portugal in 1917 when she said, "Jesus wants to establish in the world devotion to my Immaculate Heart." The Immaculate Heart of Mary is the refuge that leads all souls to heaven, and is the model of perfect love toward God and neighbor, which leads to the frequent and worthy reception of the sacraments, and inspires the faithful to make reparation for the sins committed against God and Mary's Immaculate Heart. Our Lady revealed at Fatima that the daily recitation of the Rosary, sacrifices for the conversion of sinners, and the consecration of Russia will bring about the triumph of her Immaculate Heart in which God has entrusted the peace of the world. Devotion to the Immaculate Heart of Mary is united to the Sacred Heart of Jesus, in which Jesus reigns as King in our hearts.

Prayer to Our Lady

My Queen! My Mother! I give you all of myself, and, to show my devotion to you, I consecrate to you my eyes, my ears, my mouth, my entire self. Wherefore, O loving Mother, as I am your own, keep me, defend me as your property and possession. Amen.

Heart of Mary

Sweet Heart of Mary, be my salvation! Immaculate Heart of Mary convert sinners, save souls from hell!

Consecration to Mary

Queen of the Most Holy Rosary, refuge of the human race, destroyer of all heresies! We implore thy mercy and we consecrate ourselves to thy Immaculate Heart, in union with the whole Church, and beg thee to obtain for individuals and the world the truth, justice and charity of Christ's peace. Convert unbelievers to the love of Christ and His Holy Church. May the kingdom of God triumph in the hearts and lives of men and bring glory to God through thy Immaculate Heart in union with the Heart of Jesus. Amen.

The more you honor Me, the more I will bless you.

The Infant Jesus of Prague

In the 16th century, a Spanish lady brought a valuable statue of the Infant Jesus from Spain to Bohemia when she married a Czech nobleman. Her family devoted themselves to the Child Jesus as King in their home, and in 1628, the statue was given to the Carmelites for the spread of public devotion to the Divine Infant. The statue, royally clothed and wearing a jeweled crown, was placed in Our Lady of Victory Church in Prague, and Fr. Cyril of the Mother of God helped to establish universal veneration to the Infant Jesus. Many blessings and miraculous events were granted through the devotion, and in 1655, the statue was solemnly crowned and the Infant Jesus proclaimed the Infant King of Prague. Devotion to the Infant Jesus honors the mystery of His incarnation, when God became man for the salvation of souls, instills love for Mary, the Mother of God, and inspires the faithful to live lives of humility and simplicity, with the purity and love of a child, and in fidelity to their baptismal promises. Pope Leo XIII confirmed the devotion of the Infant of Prague in 1896, favoring it with many indulgences.

The Infant Jesus of Prague

O miraculous Infant Jesus, we kneel before Your holy image and pray that You may cast Your merciful eye upon our troubled hearts. Let our prayers obtain from Your compassionate Heart the favors for which we pray from the depth of our hearts. Take from us all anxiety and despair, all that burdens us. In the name of Your Most Holy Childhood, may we find help and comfort through the Father and the Holy Spirit forever and ever. Amen.

King of Prague

O Jesus King, we crown Thee with diadem most fair. O'er all Thou reignest solely. Thy might is everywhere. With pride we tell Thy story, O wondrous Babe of Prague! With joy we sing Thy glory, O Little King of Prague!

The Infant Jesus

Infant Jesus, You live for me in the tabernacle, have mercy on my soul.

St. John Bosco and St. Dominic Savio

John Bosco was born in 1815 near Turin, Italy on a farm to poor parents. Around the age of nine, he had the desire to become a priest. During his formative years, he worked his way through school, laboring in fields and in trades, until he became a priest. After his ordination, he was assigned to take care of destitute boys, and he eventually established a home for them. He built a church and a school for his boys, and supported them from charitable donations. He taught them the importance of daily prayer, the Mass, Holy Communion and Confession, and gave them the love, discipline and fatherly trust they needed to build a good Christian character. He founded the Society of St. Francis de Sales for the care of young boys and the Daughters of Mary, Help of Christians for young girls. His Salesian motto was "give me only souls and keep all the rest." One of his students, Dominic Savio, born in 1842, founded the Company of the Immaculate Conception to help him in his work. Dominic lived a life of holiness and joy and died at the age of fourteen. St. John died on Jan. 31, 1888, and was canonized in 1934. St. Dominic was canonized in 1954.

Prayer to St. John Bosco

St. John Bosco, father and teacher of youth, raised up by God, especially for the salvation of poor and needy children; obtain that we may be enkindled by the same fire of charity as inflamed thee. Thou didst labor unceasingly in search of souls for Christ. May we, with the help of thy prayers, find God as thou didst, and enjoy eternal beatitude with thee. Amen.

St. Dominic Savio

O St. Dominic Savio, model of purity, piety, penance and apostolic zeal for youth; grant that, through your intercession, we may serve God in our ordinary duties with fervent devotion, and attain the grace of holy joy on earth, that we may one day love God forever in heaven. Amen.

St. John Vianney

St. John Vianney, known as the Curé d'Ars, was born in Dardilly, France on May 8, 1786. He worked on a farm as a shepherd, and entered the seminary at the age of twenty. After many years of rigorous study, he was ordained in 1815. Three years later, he was assigned to a parish in the remote village of Ars, where he stayed for the remainder of his life. In his love for the salvation of souls, he prayed and sacrificed to improve the spiritual life of his parishioners, which brought them to the sacraments. He had the gift of prophecy and the grace to read souls in the confessional, and soon people from around the world came to listen to him preach and to make a confession of their sins. Toward the end of his life, he spent sixteen hours a day hearing confessions. He once said, "you either belong wholly to the world or wholly to God." He was devoted to St. Philomena and was afflicted by many evil spirits. He died on Aug. 4, 1859, and was canonized in 1925. He is the patron of parish priests.

St. John Vianney

Almighty and merciful God, Thou didst make St. John Vianney wonderful by his pastoral zeal and constant prayer and penance. Grant, we beseech Thee, that by his example and intercession we may be able to win the souls of our brethren for Christ, and together with them attain to everlasting glory. Through Christ our Lord. Amen.

Prayer for Priests

O God, for the glory of Thy Majesty and the salvation of the human race, Thou didst establish St. John Vianney after Thine only-begotten Son, the supreme and eternal Priest. Grant that those whom Thy Son has chosen to be the dispensers of His divine mysteries, may, through the intercession of John Vianney, fulfill their calling for Thy glory. Amen.

St. Joseph

St. Joseph is the chaste spouse of the Blessed Virgin Mary and the foster father of Jesus Christ, God the Son made man. He was born into the family of David, and was a carpenter from Nazareth. He was betrothed to Mary, and when he found that she was carrying a child, he feared to marry her, but an angel of God told him to fear not, since she was the Mother of God. After Jesus was born, he and Mary presented Jesus in the temple. When an angel told him that Herod wanted to kill the Child Jesus, he brought Jesus and Mary into Egypt. Upon their return to Nazareth, Joseph protected and supported Jesus and Mary through his work, introducing Jesus to his trade. At the age of twelve, Jesus was absent from His parents for three days during the Passover feast, but Joseph and Mary found Him conversing with the teachers in the temple. He remained subject to Joseph and Mary in the home of the Holy Family until His public ministry. Joseph is called the "just man" who accepted, without hesitation, the joys and trials of obeying the divine will. He was proclaimed the Patron of the Universal Church in 1870, and is the patron of a happy death. His patronage includes Christian families, schools and laborers. St. Joseph faithfully guards and cares for the Church militant as he did for the Child Jesus.

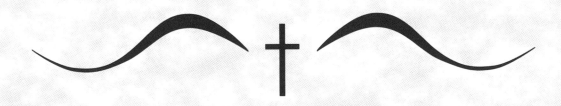

Prayer to St. Joseph

Glorious St. Joseph, faithful guardian of Jesus Christ, to you we raise our hearts and hands to implore your powerful intercession in obtaining from the Heart of Jesus all the help and graces necessary for our spiritual and temporal welfare, particularly the grace of a happy death and the special favor we now implore. O St. Joseph, accept the offering I make to you. Be my father, protector and guide in the way of salvation. Obtain for me purity of heart and a love for the spiritual life. Pray for me that I may share in the peace and joy of your holy death. Amen.

St. Joseph Moscati

Joseph Moscati was born on July 25, 1880, in Benevento, Italy to a deeply religious Catholic family. His gentleness, keen mind, and moral goodness led him to study medicine at the University of Naples, where he received his degree in 1903. Through his advanced study, he became a teacher and researcher of medicine. He took a vow of celibacy, and out of his love for Christ and charity for others, he volunteered for military service during World War I. In his lifelong practice as a doctor, he believed that the health of the body is based on the grace in the soul. Through his spiritual advice, many of his patients returned to the sacraments. He had a special love for the poor, the helpless, religious and priests, giving them treatment without charging a fee. The strength to accomplish his daily duties came from his attendance at daily Mass and his devotion to Mary. He blended his knowledge and practice of medicine with his practice of the Catholic faith. He died on April 12, 1927, and was canonized on Oct. 25, 1987.

St. Joseph Moscati

God our Father, the creator and sustainer of all life, we ask that the prayers and example of St. Joseph Moscati, Your faithful servant, a medical doctor, whose attendance at daily Mass and his devotion to Mary fortified his work of saving souls through his care for the body, may inspire those in the medical profession to serve their suffering patients with charity, understanding, self-sacrifice, and devoted treatment, especially of the unfortunate. May their service honor You, the life-giving Father in heaven, with due reverence for the sanctity of human life. Amen.

St. Jude

Jude is one of the twelve Apostles of Jesus, known as Thaddaeus. He was a brother of the Apostle James the Less, and a relative of Jesus. He preached the Gospel of Christ in Palestine, parts of the Middle East and Lybia. He wrote an epistle, instructing the Hebrew converts about the dangers of worldly ways, exhorting them to avoid ungodly deeds and to strengthen their faith in the love of God, Whose promise of eternal life is the gift of His mercy. He was martyred along with the Apostle Simon, and is the patron saint of the sick and those with helpless cases. He is traditionally portrayed with fire above his head and is holding a painting of Christ. The feast of Sts. Jude and Simon is Oct. 28.

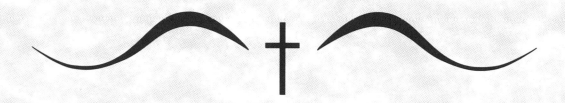

St. Jude
Patron of Impossible Cases

Glorious St. Jude, with faith in your goodness, we ask your help today. As one of Christ's chosen Apostles, you remain a pillar and foundation of His Church on earth. You are counted, we know, among the elders who always stand before God's throne. From your place of glory we know you do not forget the needs of Christ's little ones here, still struggling on the way home to God. In particular, I invoke your help with this great problem (*mention it*). Please intercede for us, gracious St. Jude, and be with us in our daily necessities. Amen.

St. Jude
Patron of Hopeless Cases

Most Holy Apostle, St. Jude, faithful servant and friend of Jesus, the Church honors and invokes you universally as the patron of hopeless cases, of things almost despaired of. Pray for me and make use, I beg you, of that singular privilege given to you to bring visible and speedy help. Come to my assistance in this great need that I may receive consolation and the help of heaven in all my difficulties, particularly (*make your request*). I promise, dear St. Jude, to honor and to gratefully encourage devotion to you as my special patron. Amen.

Blessed Kateri Tekakwitha

Kateri Tekakwitha was born in Auriesville, New York, in 1656, the daughter of a Christian mother and a Mohawk chief. She was orphaned at the age of four when her parents died of small-pox. The disease affected her sight and disfigured her face. Her uncle and two aunts adopted her. She was baptized a Catholic and received her first Holy Communion at the age of twenty, and though she was persecuted for her faith by her people, and her uncle and aunts, she remained steadfast in her beliefs. To preserve her faith, she moved to a Christian village in Canada, and there practiced her faith with great intensity through her fasting, devotion to the Eucharist, and care for the infirm. At one point she desired to become a nun. She made a solemn vow of perpetual virginity, dedicating herself completely to Christ. She died at the age of twenty-three on Apr. 17, 1680, and was beatified on June 22, 1980. She is called the Lily of the Mohawks.

Blessed Kateri Tekakwitha

Lord Jesus Christ, Your Gospel of eternal life was brought to the New World and planted along the banks of the St. Lawrence, from which blossomed forth the pure and enduring Lily, Kateri Tekakwitha. May she one day be named among the saints in Your Holy Catholic Church, and by her intercession, may we obtain the favor we ask of You as we imitate her love and devotion to Your Holy Cross and Your real presence in the Holy Eucharist. Amen.

The Last Supper

On Holy Thursday, the eve of His Passion on Calvary, Jesus Christ took bread, blessed it and gave it to His Apostles, saying, "Take and eat: THIS IS MY BODY, which will be delivered for you." Then taking the chalice into His sacred hands, He blessed it, and gave it to them saying, "Take and drink, for THIS IS THE CHALICE OF MY BLOOD, which shall be shed for you." He then said, "Do this in memory of Me." With these words, Jesus instituted the Sacrament of the Holy Eucharist, His Real Presence under the appearances of bread and wine, and conferred upon the apostles the power of His priesthood to perpetuate this Mystery of Faith for the remission of sins and to communicate His eternal life, which is necessary for the salvation of the soul. Sin had separated man from the life of God, but Jesus, God the Son made man, communicates Himself substantially to man and implants the seed of immortality and virtue in his soul through the Holy Eucharist. Through the merits of Christ's Passion, man cultivates the seed of grace and virtue sown in him through the Holy Eucharist.

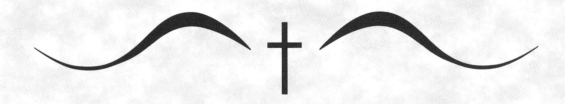

Before Holy Communion

Come, O blessed Savior, and nourish my soul with heavenly Food, the Bread of Angels, to satisfy the hunger of my soul. Come, glowing Furnace of Charity, and enkindle in my heart the flame of divine love. Come, Light of the World, and enlighten the darkness of my mind. Come, King of Kings, and make me obedient to Your holy will. Come, Good Shepherd, and take me to Yourself. Amen.

Act of Thanksgiving

I thank You, dear Lord, for Your infinite kindness in coming to me in Holy Communion. I thank You for nourishing my soul with Your Sacred Body and Most Precious Blood. May I show my gratitude to You in the Sacrament of Your love, by obedience to Your commandments, fidelity to my duties, kindness to my neighbor and to become more and more like You each day. Amen.

The Last Supper and St. John

John rested his head on the Heart of Jesus during the Last Supper. He is the beloved disciple of Jesus who, along with the other apostles, was made a priest to act in the Person of Christ. As the youngest apostle, and the disciple whom Jesus loved, he was present with Jesus at the Transfiguration, in the agony in Gethsemane, and at the foot of the cross with Mary, where Jesus entrusted Mary to his care, the Virgin to a virgin. He is the apostle of divine charity and a pillar of the Church who wrote the Fourth Gospel which reveals that Jesus is God the Word made flesh, the Bread of Life, Who commands His followers to "love as I have loved you." John is a sign of the chaste and indissoluble love of a priest that is firmly united to the Heart of Jesus, the source of all the treasures of wisdom and understanding. He loved Jesus with a pure heart. Though never martyred, he died around 104, after writing the book of the Apocalypse. His feast day is Dec. 27.

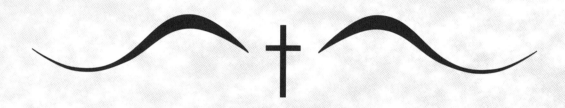

A Prayer for Priests

Keep them, I pray Thee, dearest Lord, keep them, for they are Thine - Thy priests whose lives burn out before Thy consecrated shrine. Keep them, for they are in the world, though from the world apart; when earthly pleasures tempt, allure, shelter them in Thy Heart. Keep them, and comfort them in hours of loneliness and pain, when all of their life of sacrifice for souls seems but in vain. Keep them, and O remember, Lord, they have no one but Thee, yet they have only human hearts, with human frailty. Keep them as spotless as the Host that daily they caress; their every thought and word and deed, deign, dearest Lord, to bless. Amen.

The Loaves and Fishes

The miracle of the multiplication of the five loaves and two fish that fed five thousand is testimony that Jesus has power over created nature and that He alone can satisfy man's hunger for life. He is the Shepherd of souls Who gives of Himself in multiplying the food of life. The miracle foreshadows the miracle of the Holy Eucharist, where Jesus gives His followers His Body and Blood under the appearances of bread and wine. He multiplies His real presence in the Holy Eucharist to become the Lord and King of our hearts. He feeds us with the gift and grace of Himself, and we multiply His presence in our acts of charity to those in need. Man was created to reveal himself as a gift that bears fruit and glorifies God, and when we give ourselves to Jesus, He gives us more than we need in return. In the miracle of the loaves and fishes, Jesus refreshes the body and the soul, and teaches that man does not live on bread alone, but on every word that comes from the mouth of God.

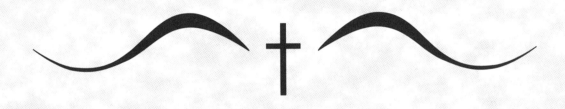

The Favors of Jesus

Dear Jesus, thank You for becoming the divine Victim to merit for me the heavenly favors of salvation. Enliven in me the faith that will increase the fruits of grace in my soul. I am grateful to You for offering Yourself to the Father on my behalf, and for all His benefits, spiritual and temporal, that have enriched my life and made me persevere in Your love and service. Amen.

Gratitude to Jesus

I thank You, most kind Jesus, for giving Yourself to me in the Holy Eucharist, with all the treasures of Your love, that there is no greater gift than You which I can receive. I am grateful that You feed and nourish my soul with Your Body and Blood, and offered Yourself in sacrifice to the Father for my salvation. Amen.

Madonna and Child

Mary is the sweet, loving Mother of Jesus, the Divine Son of God, and our spiritual mother in the order of grace. She is a merciful mother and refuge of sinners, who comforts us in our afflictions, assists us in temptation and works to reconcile us to Jesus when we commit sins. Mary is ever watchful for the salvation of our souls, and prays for us to remain faithful and to persevere in the service of her Son. Mary is the help of the living and the hope of the dying, whose name evokes lively faith, confidence and trust. She reminds us to follow the commands of her Son, and that as His followers, we are her children and the children of God the Father. Mary is the Madonna who leads the children of God safely to their true home in the kingdom of heaven.

The Memorare

Remember, O most gracious Virgin Mary, that never was it known that any one who fled to thy protection, implored thy help, or sought thy intercession, was left unaided. Inspired with this confidence, I fly unto thee, O Virgin of virgins, my Mother. To thee, I come before thee I stand, sinful and sorrowful. O Mother of the Word Incarnate! Despise not my petitions, but in thy mercy hear and answer me. Amen.

Our Blessed Mother

Sweet Mother of Jesus! Be my mother always. Make me holy, obedient, humble and a true lover of Jesus, your Son. May my life be an image of the life of Jesus, and may you guide me along the paths of life to the eternal happiness of heaven, and there be united with you who are united to God above all creatures. Dearest Madonna, give me the courage to do the will of God and enter into heaven as a true child of God. Amen.

St. Margaret Mary

Margaret Mary Alacoque was born on July 22, 1647, in Burgundy, France. From her youth, she developed a great love for Jesus in the Blessed Sacrament. She entered the Visitation order in 1671 at Paray-le-Monial and was professed the following year. Jesus appeared to her many times, revealing to her His Sacred Heart, burning as a furnace, and at other times, bleeding from the coldness and sins of men. In 1675, Jesus told her that she, along with St. Claude de le Colombière, S.J., would be instrumental in establishing and spreading public and liturgical devotion to His Sacred Heart, with its twelve promises and the practice of receiving Holy Communion on nine First Fridays. Her efforts to fulfill the instructions of Jesus met with strong opposition in her community, but eventually they accepted the devotion. Margaret Mary died on Oct. 17, 1690, and she was canonized in 1920. Devotion to the Sacred Heart was officially approved in 1765 by Pope Clement XIII.

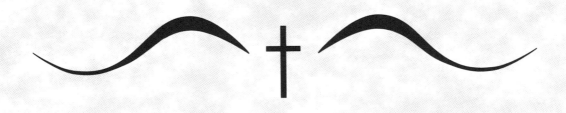

Prayer of St. Margaret Mary

Eternal Father, permit me to offer You the Heart of Jesus Christ, Your beloved Son, as He himself offered It in sacrifice to You. Receive this offering for me, as well as all the desires, sentiments, affections, movements and acts of this Sacred Heart. They are all mine since He offered Himself for me and henceforth I wish to have no other desires but His. Receive them in satisfaction for my sins, and in thanksgiving for all Your benefits. Grant me through His merits all the graces necessary for my salvation, especially that of final perseverance. Receive them as so many acts of love, adoration and praise which I offer to Your divine Majesty, since it is through the Heart of Jesus that You are worthily honored and glorified. Amen.

St. Maria Goretti

Maria was the third child of seven, born near Ancona, Italy on Oct. 16, 1890. Her father worked on a farm and brought in another man and his young son to live in his home and help on the farm. After her father died, Maria took care of the household chores, and her mother attended to the farm. One day, the youth living in their home, who previously tried to engage Maria in sinful behavior, approached her with a large dagger, and again tried to entice her to commit a sin against bodily purity. She refused, and then his lustful desires drove him to attack Maria, leaving her with several stab wounds. She was taken to a hospital, but efforts to revive her were unsuccessful. She died on July 6, 1902, after receiving Holy Communion and praying for her assailant's conversion. She was canonized on June 24, 1950, in the presence of her mother, brothers and sisters, and her assailant, who repented of his evil deed. St. Maria Goretti is a model of purity and loving obedience to God's will, winning a martyr's crown by remaining a virgin spouse of God.

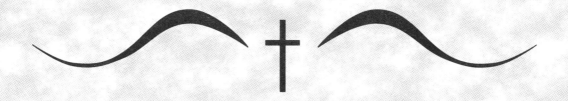

St. Maria Goretti, Patroness of Purity

We greet you, O beautiful and lovable Saint, martyr on earth and angel in heaven! Look down from your glory upon us who love and venerate you and ask God to grant us the graces we need to imitate your innocence and love of chastity. On your forehead you bear the full, brilliant and victorious name of Christ. In your virginal countenance may be read the strength of your love and the constancy of your fidelity to your Divine Spouse. As His bride, espoused in blood, you have traced in yourself His own image. To you, powerful intercessor with the Lamb of God, we entrust our sons and daughters. For, while they admire heroism, they are even more desirous of imitating your strength of faith and your inviolate purity of conduct. In you, all children will find a safe refuge, trusting that they shall be protected from every contamination, and walk the highways of life with serenity of spirit, deep joy and purity of heart. Amen.

St. Martin de Porres

Martin de Porres was born in Lima, Peru on Nov. 9, 1579, the son of a Spanish father and an Indian mother who came from Panama. Through the help of his father, he became a barber and learned to do medical work, and at fifteen he joined the Dominicans as a lay brother. He devoted himself to many penances, and had the gift of bilocation and spiritual insight with which he helped his sister, his niece and his own religious order. He cared for stray cats and dogs, and generously served the destitute, the poor and the slaves from Africa. St. Martin loved all people without discrimination, seeing that each person was created by God with an immortal soul. He was a friend of St. Rose of Lima, and he died on Nov. 3, 1639. He was canonized in 1962 and is the patron of interracial justice.

St. Martin de Porres

Most glorious Martin de Porres, whose burning charity embraced not only your needy brethren, but also the animals of the field, listen to our supplications. By imitating your virtues, may we accept the state in life that God has chosen for us, and carry our cross with courage and patience, that we may follow in the steps of Jesus and His Blessed Mother, and through His merits reach the kingdom of heaven. Amen.

Prayer for Humility

Lord, you led Martin de Porres by a life of humility to eternal glory. May we follow his example and be exalted with him in the kingdom of heaven. Through Christ our Lord. Amen.

Peace and Justice

Give peace, Lord, to those who wait for You; listen to the prayers of Your servants, and guide us in the way of justice that brings true peace. Amen.

St. Mary Magdalene

Mary Magdalene was a great sinner, who became an intimate follower of Jesus Christ and ministered to Him in Galilee, after He cast from her seven demons. She has been identified as the one who washed His feet with her tears, dried them with her hair, kissed them, and anointed them with perfume as a sign of repentance for her sins. She was with the Virgin Mary on Calvary when Jesus died, representing those who had much forgiven. The Gospels record that Jesus first appeared to her after His resurrection, and called her by name. Through the message of an angel, she announced His resurrection to the apostles. According to an ancient tradition, she lived for thirty years in a mountain-top cave, contemplating the Passion of Jesus, after Jesus ascended into heaven. Her feast day is July 22.

St. Mary Magdalene

St. Mary Magdalene! You heard from the loving lips of Jesus that your many sins were forgiven because you loved much. Pour out your love at His sacred Feet on our behalf. Your tears of repentance and of love won for you the pardon of your sins and the vision of your Risen Jesus on Easter morning. Surely, dear Saint, He who refused nothing to your love on earth, will graciously replenish us with those blessings, for which we implore your prayers. Amen.

St. Maximilian Kolbe

Maximilian Kolbe was born near Lodz, Poland on Jan. 7, 1894. His baptismal name was Raymond, and in his youth, he had a vision of Mary who offered him two crowns, one for purity and one for martyrdom, and he chose both. He then joined the Friars Minor Conventual, and took the name Maximilian. While studying for the priesthood, he founded an organization devoted to Mary Immaculate in 1917. He was ordained in Rome in 1918, and after returning to Poland, he founded a community of Franciscans dedicated to strengthening the faith and spreading devotion to Mary throughout the world. His spiritual goal was the "conquest of the whole world and every living soul for the Sacred Heart of Jesus through His Immaculate Mother." He journeyed to Japan and India to spread his message. Because of ill health, he returned to Poland, but was arrested in 1941 after the Nazis invaded Poland, and sent to a prison camp in Auschwitz, Poland. When one of the prisoners escaped, ten men were selected to die by starvation. He offered himself in the place of one who was the father of a family. He and the other prisoners endured their sufferings through prayers and sacred hymns, and, after two weeks, he was killed on Aug. 14, 1941. He was canonized by Pope John Paul II in 1982.

St. Maximilian

St. Maximilian, martyr of our age, you gave your life in place of another man. You have reflected the self-sacrifice of our Savior, and having shared His sufferings, you rejoice now in His glory. Through your prayers, we ask for the same courage to be generous in the love of God and our neighbor, and devoted to Mary Immaculate. Amen.

In Time of Trial

We thank almighty God for your virtuous life, St. Maximilian. You teach us to love our enemies and to undertake difficult tasks for the love of God as an instrument of Mary Immaculate. We ask you to pray that we may give ourselves generously to the service of God, and overcome the obstacles that overwhelm our spirit of peace and joy. Amen.

St. Michael the Archangel

St. Michael is an archangel and the captain of the armies of God. His name means "who is like unto God?" He drove out the evil army of Lucifer and his rebellious angels who made war in heaven against the will of God, and cried "we will not serve." St. Michael is the champion of the faithful in their strife with the powers of evil. All throughout history, he is the special patron and protector of those who love and follow Jesus Christ. He has guarded the chosen people of Israel, and will defend God's holy Church against the battle of the anti-christ. St. Michael is the rescuer of God's holy people against Satan and all evil spirits.

St. Michael the Archangel

St. Michael the Archangel, defend us in battle. Be our protection against the wickedness and snares of the devil. May God rebuke him, we humbly pray. And do thou, O Prince of the heavenly host, by the power of God, thrust into hell Satan and all evil spirits who wander through the world seeking the ruin of souls. Amen.

The Holy Angels

Most Holy Angels of God, protect us from the wiles of Satan and his army of deceit and evil. May Holy Michael, the archangel of God, lead the battle to defend the souls of the faithful in the time of conflict amidst the trials of this life, that through his power before God, our souls will gain the grace of eternal life, and see God face to face for all eternity. Amen.

St. Michael

St. Michael, holy archangel of God, help me to love God and to serve Him always. Amen.

St. Michael and the Blessed Virgin

From the first instant of her conception, the Blessed Virgin Mary is the Immaculate dwelling and spotless mirror of the holiness of God, more radiant than the sun itself. She is free from all sin and the tyranny of Satan in the triumph of her Immaculate Conception. She becomes the guarded sanctuary of the Holy Spirit, and the abode of Christ's humanity in which God poured forth the fullness of His grace. By the power of the Holy Spirit, She brings forth the Fruit of Life, the King of the world, Jesus Christ, Who is Lord to the glory of God the Father. St. Michael the Archangel protects the purity of Mary and defends all the children of Mary from the fury, hatred and deception of Satan, who only exists to serve himself and to make himself like God. In the battle for the salvation of souls, St. Michael casts Satan into hell and Mary's love for God crushes the proud head of Satan through the grace and power of her Immaculate Conception.

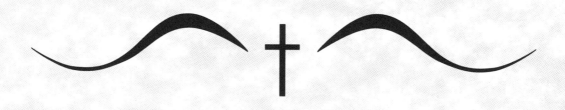

Pure Love of God

Angel of Peace! Come St. Michael, and defend the children of Mary in their battle against the evils that defile and deprive the soul of the grace of the Holy Spirit. Bear us safely by your powerful arm to our true home in heaven. Most Holy Mary, Queen of the angels and saints! Purify us in the unstained abode of your Immaculate Heart. Inflame our hearts with the love of God burning in your Heart, that we may always know and love God with all our hearts. O Holy Spirit, Spouse of Mary and Merciful Gift of the Passion of Jesus! Cleanse, illumine and sanctify our souls by Your divine grace. Pour forth the fire of Your divine love into our hearts that they may radiate a life of holiness and truth that gives glory to God in the presence of the angels and the saints forever and ever. Amen.

St. Monica and St. Augustine

Monica was born in Africa in 333. She was a Christian and married a pagan named Patricius, and had three children. With her gentleness and prayers, she endured his temper flares, and, through her example, he was baptized the year before he died. Her son, Augustine, born in 354, was educated in a Christian school, but turned to dissolute living when he entered the university in Carthage. He embraced Manichaeanism, and had a mistress for fifteen years. He taught rhetoric, and then moved to Italy. His mother, who prayed for his conversion for seventeen years, followed him to Italy. While there, Augustine was inspired by the letters of St. Paul and the sermons of St. Ambrose, and was baptized a Catholic in 387. He returned to Africa with his mother, but on the way she died. He formed a religious community and was ordained in 390. He became bishop of Hippo in 396, and zealously defended the faith from heresy. He wrote spiritual classics which influenced the Church for one thousand years. He died on Aug. 28, 430, and is one of the greatest Doctors of the Church. His mother is patroness of mothers and he is the patron of theologians.

St. Monica

Dear St. Monica, once the sorrowing mother of a wayward son, be pleased to present our petitions to our Lord in heaven. Look down upon our anxieties and needs and intercede for us as you did so fervently for Augustine. Mother of sinner-turned-saint, obtain for us patience, perseverance, and total trust in God's perfect timing. In His merciful way, may He respond to your prayers and ours which we offer through you. Amen.

Prayer of St. Augustine

O Father, light up the small duties of this day's life; may they shine with the beauty of Thy countenance. May we believe that glory can dwell in the commonest task of every day. Amen.

St. Augustine

Thou hast made us, O Lord, for Thyself and our heart shall find no rest till it rest in Thee.

The Monstrance

God's Heart is exposed through the monstrance, a sacred metal vessel, usually plated in gold or silver, that contains a consecrated Host for the exposition and procession of the Blessed Sacrament. It stands vertically and is often designed in the form of a cross, a sun burst, a church, or in an elaborate circular structure in which the consecrated Host is placed in the center in an enclosed transparent space. The Blessed Sacrament is exposed during benediction, forty hours devotion, eucharistic adoration, and is carried in procession on the feast of Corpus Christi. Many saints were devoted to the real presence of Jesus in the Blessed Sacrament, giving Him due honor and worship. In the devotion of benediction, the priest holds the monstrance with a humeral veil over his hands and blesses the people in the form of a cross.

The Divine Praises

Blessed be God. Blessed be His Holy Name. Blessed be Jesus Christ, true God and true Man. Blessed be the Name of Jesus. Blessed be His Most Sacred Heart. Blessed be His Most Precious Blood. Blessed be Jesus in the Most Holy Sacrament of the Altar. Blessed be the Holy Spirit, the Paraclete. Blessed be the great Mother of God, Mary Most Holy. Blessed be her holy and Immaculate Conception. Blessed be her glorious Assumption. Blessed the name of Mary, Virgin and Mother. Blessed be St. Joseph, her most chaste spouse. Blessed be God in His Angels and in His Saints.

I Adore Thee

Prostrate I adore Thee, Deity unseen, Who Thy glory hid beneath these shadows mean. Lo, to Thee surrendered, my whole heart is bowed, tranced as it beholds Thee, shrined within the cloud.

O Saving Victim

O saving Victim, opening wide the gate of heaven to man below, our foes press on from every side: Thine aid supply, Thy strength bestow.

The Most Holy Trinity

The Most Holy Trinity is the Divine mystery of the uncreated, undivided and unchanging unity of the one only God in Three Divine Persons, the fundamental dogma of the Catholic Church, revealed by Jesus Christ, the Second Divine Person made man. The First Person, God the Father, eternally begets God the Son, the Second Person, and God the Holy Spirit proceeds from the love of the Father and the Son. Each Person in God is absolute, eternal and distinct, and each Person is God. The salvation of each soul depends on baptism into the life of the Holy Trinity, and perseverance in the grace of redemption in Jesus Christ that unites the soul to the Triune God. The Church has defined the doctrine of the Trinity against heresies that deny the consubstantial union of God the Father with God the Son Who became man. The mystery of the Three Persons in one God in the Most Holy Trinity is a truth that is only known through Divine Revelation.

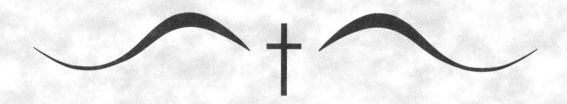

The Most Holy Trinity

Glory be to the Father, Who by His almighty power and love created me, making me in the image and likeness of God. Glory be to the Son, Who by His Precious Blood delivered me from hell, and opened for me the gates of heaven. Glory be to the Holy Spirit, Who has sanctified me in the sacrament of Baptism, and continues to sanctify me by the graces I receive daily from His bounty. Glory be to the Three adorable Persons of the Most Holy Trinity. Amen.

Act of Faith

O my God, I firmly believe in one God, in three divine Persons, the Father, the Son and the Holy Spirit. I believe in Jesus Christ, the true and only Son of God, Who was born of the Virgin Mary and died on the cross for our salvation. I believe all the sacred truths that the Holy Catholic Church teaches because they have been revealed by You, Who can neither deceive nor be deceived. Amen.

Our Lady of Grace

Our Lady of Grace, the Mother of God conceived without sin and the vanquisher of the devil, is the channel of divine grace and the spiritual mother of mankind in the order of grace. She appeared three times in 1830 as Mary Immaculate to Catherine Labouré, a Daughter of Charity, who was born May 2, 1806, and entered the convent in Paris, France, in 1830. On Nov. 27, 1830, Our Lady appeared to her and was standing on a white globe, with rings on her fingers that radiated different rays of light, and represented the power of her intercession. Around her was a message that read: "O Mary, conceived without sin, pray for us who have recourse to thee." She asked to have a medal struck after this image, with the reverse side showing a cross and a bar above a large M, and the Hearts of Jesus and Mary below it, one crowned with thorns and the other pierced with a sword. She said that all who wear it would receive great graces. The medal was made and then widely distributed, with many graces bestowed on the faithful. It was known as the Medal of the Immaculate Conception, and later became known as the Miraculous Medal. St. Catherine died on Dec. 31, 1876, and was canonized in 1947.

Our Lady of the Miraculous Medal

Virgin Mother of God, Mary Immaculate , I unite myself to you under your title of Our Lady of the Miraculous Medal. May this medal be for me a sure sign of your motherly affection for me and a constant reminder of my filial duties toward you. While wearing it, may I be blessed by your loving protection and preserved in the grace of your Son. Most powerful Virgin, Mother of our Savior, keep me close to you every moment of my life, so that like you I may live and act according to the example of your Son. Amen.

Our Lady of Grace

O Mary, conceived without sin, pray for us who have recourse to thee.

Our Lady of Guadalupe

Our Lady of Guadalupe, the Virgin Mary and merciful mother of the living God, appeared on Dec. 9, 1531, in Tepeyac, Mexico to an Indian convert named Juan Diego, while he was on his way to early morning Mass on the Spanish feast of the Immaculate Conception. She asked that a church be built there on the hill, and that he should seek the help of the bishop. After two visits to the bishop, Juan told Mary that he needed a sign, and she promised to provide one the next day. But because of his very sick uncle, Juan only met Mary on Dec. 12, as he went to find a priest to give his uncle the Last Sacraments. Mary told Juan that she had cured his uncle, and that he should gather the roses blooming on the hillside into his tilma, and after she arranged them, to present them to the bishop as her sign. When he opened his tilma before the bishop, they saw the roses and a beautiful portrait of Our Lady imprinted on the tilma. With this sign, the bishop ordered the construction of a church in honor of Mary. Many conversions occurred through the miraculous image of her Immaculate Conception. She is called Our Lady of Guadalupe, the one who "crushes the stone serpent," and is the Patroness of the Americas. Her feast is Dec. 12.

Our Lady of Guadalupe

Our Lady of Guadalupe, mystical rose, make intercession for Holy Church, protect the Sovereign Pontiff, help all those who invoke thee in their necessities, and since thou art the ever Virgin Mary and Mother of the true God, obtain for us from thy most holy Son the grace of keeping our faith, sweet hope in the midst of the bitterness of life, burning charity and the precious gift of final perseverance. Amen.

Virgin of Guadalupe

Virgin of Guadalupe, Mother of the Americas, we pray to you for all the Bishops, that they may lead the faithful along paths of intense Christian life, of love and humble service of God and souls. Grant to our homes the grace of loving and respecting life in its beginnings, with the same love with which you conceived in your womb the life of the Son of God. Amen.

Padre Pio

Padre Pio was born on May 25, 1887, in the humble surroundings of Pietrelcina, Italy. He joined the Capuchin Franciscans in 1903, and was ordained in 1910. He taught in the seminary, and on Sept. 20, 1918, he received the stigmata, the bleeding wounds of Christ's Passion in his hands, feet and side. He had the gift of prophecy, healing, bilocation, the odor of sanctity, and could read the souls of penitents in the confessional. He led many souls to a permanent conversion, and others to ask for God's forgiveness with their whole heart. He was accused of being a fraud, but the charges proved to be unfounded. Padre Pio was a heroic, generous priest who prayed and sacrificed for the salvation of souls and offered himself as a victim for sinners and for the souls in Purgatory. He prayed to his guardian angel that sinners would love Mary. In 1947, he helped to establish a Home for the Relief of the Suffering. He defended the papal teaching *Humanae Vitae* prohibiting birth control, and died on Sept. 23, 1968, a humble self-effacing friar whose life of holiness and sacrifice brought many souls to the love of Christ.

Padre Pio

O Lord, we ask for a boundless confidence and trust in Your divine mercy, and the courage to accept the crosses and sufferings which bring immense goodness to our souls and that of Your Church. Help us to love You with a pure and contrite heart, and to humble ourselves beneath Your cross, as we climb the mountain of holiness, carrying our cross that leads to heavenly glory. May we receive You with great faith and love in Holy Communion, and allow You to act in us as You desire for Your greater glory. O Jesus, most adorable Heart and eternal fountain of Divine Love, may our prayer find favor before the Divine Majesty of Your heavenly Father. Amen.

St. Patrick

Patrick was born in Scotland around 387. As a youth, he was taken into slavery and sent to pagan Ireland. There he tended sheep, and during his six years in captivity he prayed to God so that "the love of God and His fear grew in me more and more, as did the faith." In a vision, he was told to flee Ireland. After he returned home safely, he was advised to study for the priesthood in France, where he met St. Germanus, who gave him spiritual direction. He was ordained, and, later on, Pope St. Celestine sent him to preach the Gospel in Ireland. He was made a bishop, and his mission began in Northern Ireland, where he had been a slave. His preaching and miracles converted many pagans, including a king and twelve thousand of his subjects. He told one pagan ruler that the three Persons in one God are like the three leaves in a shamrock. Patrick ordained priests, consecrated virgins, established monasteries, built churches. He lived to save souls for Christ. He endured many hardships in his missionary work. In thirty years of labor for Christ, he converted Ireland to the Catholic faith, so that "the sons and daughters of the kings of the Irish are seen to be monks and virgins of Christ." Patrick died on Mar. 17, 461. He is called the "Apostle of Ireland."

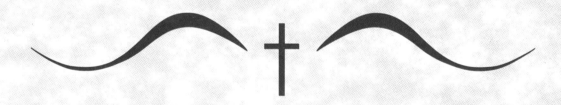

St. Patrick's Breastplate

Christ as a light, illumine and guide me! Christ as a shield, o'ershadow and cover me! Christ be under me! Christ be over me! Christ be before me, behind me, and about me! Christ be this day within and without me! Christ, lowly and meek; Christ, all-powerful, be in the hearts of all to whom I speak, on the lips of all who speak to me.

St. Patrick

God our Father, You sent St. Patrick to preach Your glory to the people of Ireland. By the help of his prayers, may all Christians proclaim Your love to all people. Through Christ our Lord. Amen.

St. Paul

Paul, born with the name Saul, was a Pharisee from Tarsus in Cilcia, who became a Roman citizen, and was educated in Jerusalem. He was an enemy of Christians, and supported the stoning of St. Stephen, the first Christian martyr. On his way to Damascus around the year 35 to persecute Christians, he had a vision of Jesus, and was converted to the Christian faith, and commissioned as the Apostle to the Gentiles. After his baptism, he took the name Paul, learned the faith, and then began preaching about Jesus. He met the apostles, assisted them, and then journeyed with a disciple named Barnabas to Asia Minor and Europe, establishing churches and making converts. He was persecuted and suffered much in his journeys to spread the Gospel of Christ. He attended the Council in Jerusalem which decided that uncircumcised converts could be baptized. Paul spent three years preaching in Ephesus, and on his return to Jerusalem, he was arrested and later sent to Rome for his trial. According to ancient tradition, he went to Spain after his prison release, and upon his return to Rome in 67, he was beheaded the same day that St. Peter was martyred. He wrote fourteen letters which are part of the sacred deposit of the faith and is co-founder with St. Peter of the Church in Rome.

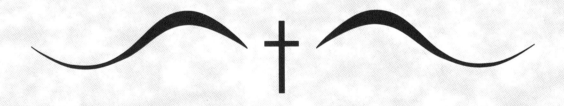

Prayer to St. Paul

Glorious St. Paul, from being a persecutor of the Christian name, you became its most zealous apostle. To make Jesus, our Divine Savior, known to the uttermost parts of the earth, you suffered prison, scourgings, stonings, shipwreck, and all manner of persecution, and shed the last drop of your blood. Obtain for us the grace to accept the infirmities, sufferings and misfortunes of this life as favors of the divine mercy. So may we never grow weary of the trials of our exile, but rather show ourselves ever more faithful and fervent. Amen.

St. Peregrine

Peregrine was born in 1260 at Forlì, Italy to an affluent family. He lived a comfortable life as a youth, and politically opposed the papacy. After he experienced the forgiveness of St. Philip Benizi, he changed his life and joined the Servite order. He was ordained a priest, and later returned to his home to establish a Servite community. There he was widely known for his preaching, penances, and counsel in the confessional. He was cured of cancer, after he received a vision of Christ on the cross reaching out His hand to touch his impaired limb. He died in 1345 and was canonized in 1726. He is the patron of cancer patients.

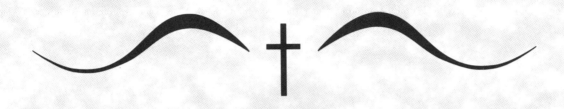

St. Peregrine
Patron of Cancer Patients

O glorious and faithful St. Peregrine, you answered the divine call with a ready spirit, forsaking all the comforts of a life of ease and all the empty honors of the world, to dedicate yourself to God in the order of His most holy Mother. You labored for the salvation of souls, and in union with Jesus Crucified, you endured the most painful sufferings from an incurable wound with such patience as to deserve to be healed miraculously by Him with a touch of His divine hand. Intercede for us, that if it be God's holy will, we may also be delivered from the infirmities that now afflict our bodies. Above all obtain for us the grace of perfect resignation to any suffering which it shall please Him to send us. Obtain for us, we pray, the grace to answer every call from God. Enkindle in our hearts a consuming zeal for the salvation of souls, so that, by imitating your virtues and tenderly loving our crucified Lord and His sorrowing Mother, we may be enabled to merit glory everlasting in paradise. Amen.

St. Peter

Peter, named Simon, was a fisherman from Galilee. His brother Andrew introduced him to Jesus, Who changed his name to Peter. He left his family and worldly possessions to become one of His chosen apostles. When Peter declared that Jesus is "Christ, the Son of the living God," Jesus confirmed that "thou art Peter, and upon this rock I will build My Church, and the gates of hell shall not prevail against it." Jesus entrusted Peter with the keys of the kingdom of heaven. He was a witness to the teaching and miracles of Jesus, yet denied Him three times after Jesus was arrested by Roman soldiers. After His resurrection, Jesus made Peter His Vicar, commanding Him to "feed My lambs." Peter converted many by his preaching and miracles in the name of Jesus Christ. After the martyrdom of the Apostle James, Peter was imprisoned by Herod, but was released by an angel. He presided at the Council of Jerusalem, which declared that converts were not subject to the law of circumcision. He founded the Church in Rome, was its first Bishop, and during the reign of Nero, around 67, was crucified upside down on Vatican Hill. Peter is the Prince of the Apostles, and the rock and foundation of unity in Christ's Catholic Church.

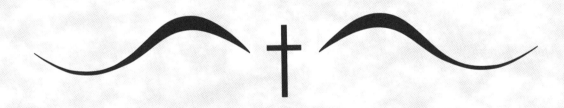

Novena to St. Peter

O Holy Apostle, St. Peter, because you are the Rock upon which Almighty God has built His Church; obtain for me I pray you, lively faith, firm hope and burning love; complete detachment from myself, contempt of the world, patience in adversity, humility in prosperity, recollection in prayer, purity of heart, a right intention in all my works, diligence in fulfilling the duties of my state of life, constancy in my resolutions, resignation to the will of God and perseverance to the will of God even unto death; that so, by means of your intercession and your glorious merits, I may be made worthy to appear before the chief and eternal Shepherd of souls, Jesus Christ, Who with the Father and the Holy Spirit lives and reigns for ever. Amen.

St. Pius X

Pope St. Pius X, born Joseph Sarto on June 2, 1835, was raised in a poor family near Trevino, Italy. In his youth, he walked to school barefoot to preserve his shoes. He entered the seminary in Padua in 1850 and was ordained in 1858. In 1884, he was made the bishop of Mantua, and in 1893 was named cardinal Patriarch of Venice. He was elected Pope on Aug. 4, 1904, and his motto was "to restore all things in Christ." During his reign, he revised the Divine Office, initiated the codifying of canon law, and taught that children must know their catechism, should receive Holy Communion often, and receive their First Holy Communion after reaching the age of reason. He wrote an encyclical condemning the heresy of modernism, and required priests to take an oath against it. He died on Aug. 20, 1914, and in his will he said, "I was born poor; I lived poor; I wish to die poor." He was canonized by Pope Pius XII in 1954.

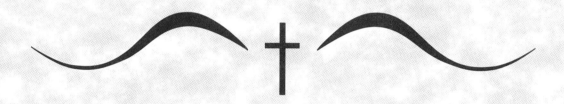

St. Pius X Prayer for Daily Communion

O most sweet Jesus, Who has come into this world to give all souls the life of Thy grace, and Who, to preserve and increase it in them, has willed to be the daily Remedy of their infirmity and the Food for each day, we humbly beg Thee— by Thy Heart so burning with love for us— to pour Thy Divine Spirit upon all souls in order that those who have the misfortune to be in the state of mortal sin may, returning to Thee, find the life of grace which they have lost. And grant that those who are already living by this divine life may devoutly approach Thy divine table every day when it is possible, so that receiving each day in Holy Communion the antidote of their daily venial sins, and each day sustaining in themselves the life of Thy grace and thus ever purifying themselves the more, they may finally come to a happy life with Thee. Amen.

The Presentation of Mary

Ancient tradition teaches that the Blessed Virgin Mary was presented and solemnly offered to God in the temple of Jerusalem at the age of three. Her parents, Sts. Joachim and Ann, consecrated her to God through the hands of a priest in the temple, and she was brought up by the holy women living at the temple in the love and service of God. Her soul was adorned with the special grace of her Immaculate Conception to the praise of the holy angels, and to the glory of the Most Holy Trinity. The Father looked upon her as His beloved Daughter, the Son saw her as His holy Mother, and the Holy Spirit as His Immaculate Spouse. Mary was the Daughter of Zion, the temple of the Lord, chosen by God as the model of virginity, and her presentation to God has inspired all virgins who have followed her example down through the ages. The feast of the Presentation was celebrated in the East in the 6th century, and it was extended to the universal Church by Pope Sixtus V in 1585.

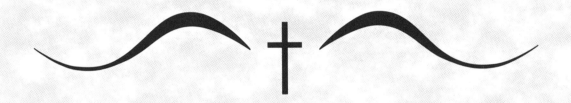

The Presentation of Mary

O God, You were pleased that Blessed Mary, ever a virgin, the dwelling place of the Holy Spirit, should be presented in the temple. Grant, we pray, that through her prayers we may be found worthy to be presented in the temple where You dwell in glory. We ask this through Christ our Lord. Amen.

The Virgin Mary

Blessed are you, Mary, because you believed that the Lord's words to you would be fulfilled. Holy Mother of God, Mary ever-Virgin, you are the temple of the Lord and the dwelling place of the Holy Spirit. Beyond all others you were pleasing to our Lord Jesus Christ. May we follow your Son with a pure heart. Amen.

The Holiness of Mary

After her shall virgins be brought to the King.

The Priest and the Mass

Jesus Christ instituted the priesthood at the Last Supper to continue His sacrifice on Calvary in the Holy Sacrifice of the Mass, which is the sacrifice of Calvary sacramentally re-enacted in an unbloody manner. Through the priest, acting in the Person of Christ, Jesus offers Himself as Priest and Victim, along with the offering of the faithful, to His Father in heaven, and gives us the graces He merited for our salvation when He shed His Precious Blood to free us from the slavery of sin. Jesus, both God and Man, gives His priests the power to change bread and wine into the sacrifice and sacrament of His Body and Blood. At the Consecration of the Mass, the sacrifice of Calvary in all its glory is made present, and the faithful enter into the life-giving sacrifice of Jesus, and merit the grace to receive His glorified Body and Blood into their souls in Holy Communion. Jesus thirsts for our love, and under the appearances of bread and wine in the Holy Sacrifice of the Mass, we love Him in His real presence through the priest.

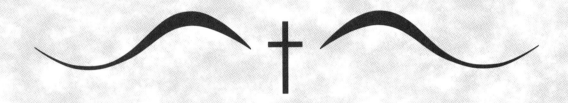

Obsecro Te

I beseech Thee, most sweet Lord Jesus Christ, to grant that Thy Passion may be to me a power by which I may be strengthened, protected and defended. May Thy wounds be to me food and drink, by which I may be nourished, inebriated and overjoyed. May the sprinkling of Thy Blood be to me the washing away of all my sins. May Thy death prove to me life eternal, Thy cross be to me an everlasting glory. In these be my refreshment, my joy, my preservation and sweetness of heart. Amen.

The Precious Blood

Eternal Father, we offer You the Precious Blood of Jesus, poured out on the cross and offered daily on the altar, for those who are to die this day, for the souls in purgatory, and for our final union with Christ in glory. Amen.

The Sacred Heart of Jesus

From the pierced Heart of Jesus, the Redeemer of man, the Church was born and nourished by the Precious Blood flowing forth from His Sacred Heart. Many saints were inflamed with the love of the Heart of Jesus, the oratory of God's divine love, and great impetus was given to It through the preaching of St. John Eudes and the revelations of Jesus to St. Margaret Mary Alacoque. Devotion to the Sacred Heart of Jesus, present in the Blessed Sacrament, is an outgrowth of devotion to His sacred humanity, and is the worship of the unfathomable riches of His love, mercy, grace, and sanctification for the salvation of souls. It draws men away from the dominion of Satan, and brings them under the rule of Christ's love. The love of Jesus with one's whole heart and soul perfectly responds to the merciful love in the Heart of Jesus, and seeks to make reparation to His Sacred Heart for all the outrages committed against It. Devotion to the Sacred Heart of Jesus was approved for the universal Church on Aug. 23, 1856, by Pope Pius IX.

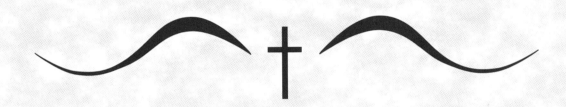

Redeemer of the World

Sacred Heart of Jesus, through Your redeeming love, enkindle in my heart that divine fire which consumes the saints and transforms them into You. O Heart of the living God, Light of the world, I adore You; for You I live and die. O Jesus, Life eternal in the bosom of the Father, Life of souls made in Your likeness, in the name of Your love reveal Your Heart and make It known through me. Amen.

The Sacred Heart

Eternal Father I offer Thee the Sacred Heart of Jesus, with all the love, sufferings and merits It possesses, to make reparation for my sins, and to supply for the good I did not do to love Thee in the Heart of Jesus. Amen.

The Heart of Jesus

Jesus, meek and humble of Heart, make our hearts like unto Thine.

St. Simon Stock

Simon Stock was born in Kent, England and became a hermit at the age of twelve, living in prayer and penance in the trunk or stock of a tree. He joined the Carmelite order in the Holy Land, but returned to England after the order was forced out. He was made the prior-general in 1245, and established many Carmelite houses in Europe. When persecution arose against his order, he prayed for the help of the Blessed Virgin Mary. She appeared to him on July 16, 1251, and gave him a Brown Scapular, promising that those who wear it will have her protection and will not suffer eternal fire. The devotion of the Brown Scapular rapidly spread throughout the Church, and the Holy See enriched it with many indulgences. Numerous miracles of conversion are attributed to it through the prayers of Mary. The Brown Scapular is the garment of grace for the soul, which, through the intercession of Mary, overcomes sin and clothes the soul with the wedding garment of heaven. Mary appeared to St. Simon as Our Lady of Mount Carmel, because she is the garden of holiness in which blossoms forth true faith in God. She appeared again in 1917 in a vision of the Brown Scapular at Fatima. St. Simon died on May 16, 1265, and the feast of Our Lady of Mount Carmel is celebrated on July 16.

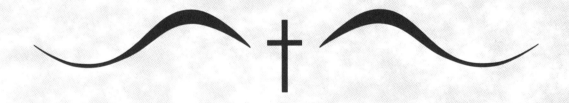

Our Lady of Mount Carmel

O Most beautiful Flower of Mount Carmel, most fruitful Vine, splendor of Heaven, Holy Mother of the Son of God, Immaculate Virgin Mother, assist me in this my necessity. O Star of the Sea, help me and show me that you are my Mother. O Holy Mary, Mother of God, Queen of Heaven and earth, I humbly beseech you from the bottom of my heart, to succor me in this necessity; there are none that can withstand your power. O Mary, conceived without sin, pray for us who have recourse to thee (3 times). Sweet Mother, I place this cause in thy hands (3 times).

Fr. Solanus Casey

Fr. Solanus Casey, born Bernard Casey on Nov. 25, 1870, was raised in Prescott, Wisconsin, on a family farm. He was the sixth of sixteen children, and worked on the farm, completing grade school only in 1887. He then supported his family by working in Stillwater, Minnesota, in a log mill, a kiln and as a prison guard and streetcar driver. After his family moved to Superior, Wisconsin, he decided to become a priest, and eventually was accepted by the Capuchins in Detroit, despite his academic difficulties. He was ordained a priest on July 24, 1904, as a simplex priest without the permission to give formal sermons or hear confessions. He was assigned the duty of sacristan and porter. He advised those he met to receive the sacraments, trust in God and do penance for sins. He enrolled many of them in the Seraphic Mass Association, and asked them to show their gratitude to God in deeds of charity for any favors granted. Many people testified to the healing and prophetic power of Christ working through Fr. Solanus. He was especially generous to the poor and opened a soup kitchen for them in 1946. He was devoted to the Little Flower and Our Lady, and believed in thanking God at all times. He died on July 31, 1957.

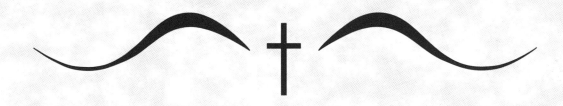

Fr. Solanus Casey

Lord Jesus, help us to thank You at all times for the crosses and blessings that You send to us for the salvation of our soul, and with confidence in Your Divine Wisdom, may we patiently and humbly accept Your divine plans with courage as did Fr. Solanus Casey. May You grant us the favor we ask and relief from any illness if it brings greater honor and glory to You. Amen.

St. Therese of the Child Jesus

St. Therese, the Little Flower, was born on Jan. 2, 1873, in Alençon, France, the youngest of nine children of a watchmaker. After her mother died, the family moved to Lisieux, where two of her sisters entered the Carmelite convent. At the age of fifteen, she was admitted to the same convent, and made her profession in 1890, taking the name of Therese of the Child Jesus. She was stricken with the disease of tuberculosis, but endured her sufferings with heroic patience and courage, offering them for the salvation of souls. She is known for her "little way of spiritual childhood," of accepting with the simplicity and trust of a child God's will, and the crosses of daily life out of love for God. She became mistress of novices in 1895 and, on Sept. 30, 1897, died at the age of twenty-four. She is one of the most popular of the modern saints who said "I will spend my heaven doing good on earth." She was canonized in 1925 and was made patron saint of the missions along with St. Francis Xavier.

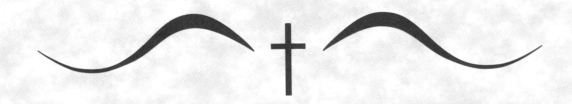

Prayer to St. Therese

O Little Therese of the Child Jesus who during your short life became a mirror of angelic purity, love of God and wholehearted abandonment to His will, plead my case before His Holy Throne. You promised to spend your Heaven doing good upon earth. Intercede for me in my hour of need (*mention the grace desired*), if it is for the greater glory of God and the good of my soul. Dear St. Therese, obtain for me the blessings I need to attain my salvation. Amen.

The Little Flower

Dear Little Flower of Carmel! By love and suffering on earth, you won the power with God which you now enjoy in heaven. From there, you have showered down countless blessings and miracles on this poor world by the power of your divine Spouse. You are the missionary of love. Obtain for us the grace to love Jesus more, and all others for His sake. I thank the Most Holy Trinity for the blessings conferred upon the world through your prayers. Amen.

St. Thomas

Thomas, surnamed the twin, was a fisherman from Galilee whom Jesus called to be one of His apostles. He encouraged the other apostles to follow Jesus even if it meant their death, but at the Last Supper, he did not understand where Jesus was going to prepare a place for them. Thomas doubted in the resurrection of Jesus, even though the other apostles had seen Him on Easter Sunday. He saw Jesus eight days later with the rest of the apostles in the Upper Room, and when he placed his fingers in the nailprints of His hands, and his hand in His pierced side, Thomas said, "My Lord and my God!" The faith of Thomas confirmed that Jesus had truly risen from the dead and that Jesus Christ is truly God, a testimony for all Christians who are called to believe in Jesus without ever having seen Him. After Pentecost, according to an ancient tradition, Thomas preached the Gospel in southern India, where he was martyred for his faith in Christ.

St. Thomas the Apostle

O God, You sent Your Son into the world to bring the light of divine Truth to a fallen world. Grant, through the intercession of St. Thomas, the Apostle, the grace of conversion and perseverance in the lives of many souls, and, by the inspiration of his faith in the resurrection of Your Son from the dead, a firm belief in the divinity of Jesus Christ and docility to the tradition and authority of His Holy Church. Amen.

St. Thomas More

Thomas More was born in London, England, on Feb. 6, 1478, the son of lawyer and judge. He studied law at Oxford and became a lawyer in 1501, and was a member of the English Parliament. He was married in 1505, had four children, and when his wife died, he married a widow in 1511. He carried on a religious and intellectual life in his home, led the family prayers and was the friend of the clergy, scholars and the poor. He was a man of wit and humor who studied the classics, played a lute, and wrote a world renowned book, *Utopia*, which prompted King Henry VIII to employ his services in high positions. He was made Lord Chancellor in 1529, but resigned his post in 1532 when the King made himself the Head of the Church of England in defiance of the Pope who refused to annul his marriage. Thomas retired to a simple family life, but was accused of treason when he refused to take an oath acknowledging the supremacy of the King in the Church of England. He was imprisoned in the Tower of London, and then beheaded on July 6, 1535. He was canonized in 1935 and is the patron of lawyers.

St. Thomas More, Patron of Catholic Lawyers

O glorious, merry martyr, St. Thomas More! Your constant prayer was that your heart should never grow cold or lukewarm in love for your sweet Savior, Jesus! With noble charity for your enemies, you went to your martyrdom with a kindly jest on your lips, pray for us, that we may obtain the grace which was your glory, of cheerful giving both to God and man.

From your glory on high, intercede for us that we may join you in the company of the saints and rejoice with Him Who won our salvation through His bitter Passion and Death. May your prayers to Christ the King guide those who work in the legal profession to learn from you that service to others is inseparable from the laws of God and His Holy Church. Amen.

The Wound in the Shoulder

Wounded, despised, forsaken and rejected, Our Savior, Jesus Christ, carried the cross of salvation that bore the weight of the sins of the world. Our Lord told St. Bernard that the Wound in His shoulder on which he carried His cross was the most painful one of His Passion. Out of love for sinners, Jesus carried the heavy cross to make satisfaction to the Father for our sins. His Wound in the shoulder, caused by our sins, pleas for the mercy of God which reconciles us to the Father. The Precious Blood flowing from His shoulder lightens our burdens and alleviates our sufferings. Through His cross, Jesus teaches us to carry the burdens of one another and become the blessed of His Father. In carrying our cross with Jesus, we partake in the humility, patience and charity of His love that glorifies the Father and leads to the kingdom of heaven. Devotion to the Wound in the shoulder of Jesus merits for us the remission of our sins, brings peace to our soul, and makes reparation for our sins and the sins of the whole world.

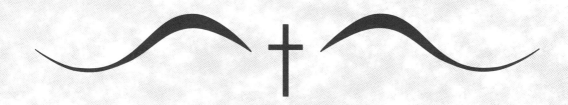

Prayer to the Wound in the Shoulder

O most loving Jesus, meek Lamb of God, I, a miserable sinner, salute and worship the most Sacred Wound of Thy Shoulder on which Thou didst bear Thy heavy cross, which so tore Thy flesh and laid bare Thy bones as to inflict on Thee an anguish greater than any other wound of Thy most blessed body. I adore Thee, O Jesus most sorrowful; I praise and glorify Thee, and give Thee thanks for this most sacred and painful Wound, beseeching Thee by that exceeding pain, and by the crushing burden of Thy heavy cross, to be merciful to me, a sinner, to forgive me all my mortal and venial sins, and to lead me on toward heaven along the Way of Thy Cross. Amen.

A
Holy Card
Prayer Book II

A Compilation of Saints and Holy People

Text
Leaflet Missal Company Staff

Artist
Anna May McCallum

The Leaflet Missal Company
976 West Minnehaha Avenue Saint Paul, Minnesota 55104

Printed in U.S.A.

Nihil Obstat:

Richard J. Schuler
Censor Deputatus

Imprimatur:

✢ John R. Roach, D.D.
Archbishop of St. Paul and Minneapolis

ISBN: 1-885845-01-4

Published, printed and bound in U.S.A.

THE LEAFLET MISSAL COMPANY
976 W. Minnehaha Ave.
St. Paul, MN 55104

Dedication

We dedicate this book to the Good Shepherd Who lays down His life for His sheep and feeds them with His Body and Blood that they will follow the voice of His word and have eternal life in the pasture of heaven.

Table of Contents

The Annunciation

THE ANNUNCIATION OF THE BLESSED VIRGIN MARY is the announcement from the angel Gabriel to Mary that she, who was full of grace, was chosen to be the Mother of God. Mary responds to God's proposal of the mystery of the Incarnation and, in the name of all humanity, says, "behold the handmaid of the Lord; be it done unto me according to Thy word." Through her free consent, God the Son descends from heaven to earth to dwell in the incorruptible paradise of her Immaculate Heart. At the message of the angel, she becomes the Mother of God made man, He Who is true God and true Man, and unconditionally accepts the gift of divine motherhood for the salvation of the world. Through the power of the Holy Spirit, she becomes the new ark of the covenant revealing God's glory and contains the true Manna of heaven, the divine Holy of Holies in the sanctuary of her radiant Heart. Mary's faith undid Eve's rejection of the word of God and conceived the sinless Lamb of God that made her the fruitful bride of God that would bring forth sons and daughters who are born through the redeeming grace of God.

The Angelus

V. The angel of the Lord declared unto Mary. *R.* And she conceived of the Holy Spirit. Hail Mary, etc. *V.* Behold the handmaid of the Lord. *R.* Be it done unto me according to thy word. Hail Mary, etc. *V.* And the Word was made Flesh. *R.* And dwelt among us. Hail Mary, etc. *V.* Pray for us, O holy Mother of God. *R.* That we may be made worthy of the promises of Christ.

Let us Pray:

Pour forth, we beseech Thee, O Lord, Thy grace into our hearts, that we to whom the Incarnation of Christ, Thy Son, was made known by the message of an angel, may by His Passion and Cross, be brought to the glory of His Resurrection. Through the same Christ our Lord. Amen.

Blessed Josephine Bakhita, pray for us!

Blessed Josephine Bakhita

JOSEPHINE BAKHITA was born in 1869 in the area of Darfur in the Sudan. She had three brothers and four sisters. At the age of nine, she was kidnapped and sold to slave merchants, never to see her family again. Her captors named her Bakhita, meaning "lucky one." She was moved with other slaves in walking caravans across desert and forest land, having a padlocked chain around her neck. She worked for an Arabian chief, but after disappointing him, she was beaten and sold to a Turkish general, serving him for three years and receiving a daily punishment. She was scourged by his soldiers and once cruelly tattooed. She was then sold to an Italian master in Khartoum who sent her to Italy to be a nursemaid. An administrator of her master in Venice helped her to enter a boarding school run by the Canossian sisters where she came to know "God whom I had experienced in my soul since childhood without knowing Who He was." She took instructions in the Catholic faith, and, "with a joy that only the angels could describe," was baptized with the name of Josephine, confirmed and received her First Holy Communion from the Cardinal Patriarch of Venice on Jan. 9, 1890. She was accepted into the religious life by Cardinal Giuseppe Sarto, the future St. Pius X, and became a Canossian Daughter of Charity on Dec. 8, 1896. She died on Feb.8, 1947 and was beatified by Pope John Paul II on May 17, 1992, who honored her on her own soil during his pastoral visit to Khartoum on Feb. 10, 1993.

Prayer to Blessed Josephine

God the Father of Mercy, You have given us the splendid gift of Blessed Josephine Bakhita, a shining example of the spirit of the beatitudes. Through her intercession may we obey You with a happy heart, and reach out to all people to bring them the light of faith, that we may belong to You alone. Through Christ our Lord. Amen.

St. Bridget of Sweden, pray for us!

St. Bridget of Sweden

BRIDGET was born in 1303 to a wealthy Swedish family. In obedience to the wishes of her father, she was married at the age of fourteen to a prince. She raised eight children, one of whom became St. Catherine of Sweden. After twenty-eight years of marriage, her husband died and she relinquished her title of princess and founded an order devoted to the Most Holy Savior. She led pilgrimages to Rome and the Holy Land out of her love for the sufferings of Christ. She reformed monasteries and worked to restore the papal throne to Rome. On numerous occasions, she denounced the evil ways of public officials. Bridget received prophetic insights and visions and wrote fifteen magnificent prayers on the Passion of Jesus. She said that Jesus was the "mirror of eternal splendor...the treasure of every real good and every joy." She prayed that Christ's sufferings "be renewed in my soul." She died in Rome in 1373 and was canonized in 1391. She is the patroness of Sweden.

St. Bridget, Widow

O Lord our God, Who revealed through Thy Son heavenly messages to Thy servant Bridget, grant that we, by her intercession, may renounce the comforts of the world to follow Thy Son's Word and glory in His Cross and so come to the full revelation of Thy glory in heaven. Through Christ our Lord. Amen.

Prayer to St. Bridget

O St. Bridget, by your devotion to the Passion and Death of Jesus Christ, may I resist the world, the flesh and the devil that the fruits of His sufferings may be renewed in my soul and I will live for God and have true contrition and remission of all my sins. In the name of Jesus Christ the Lord. Amen.

Our Lady of Mount Carmel

OUR LADY OF MOUNT CARMEL is the patronal feast of Carmelites that is celebrated on July 16. She appeared to St. Simon Stock, a Carmelite, on July 16, 1251, holding in her hand a Brown Scapular, and promised him that those who wear it shall not suffer eternal fire. According to tradition, those who faithfully wear the Brown Scapular, observe chastity according to their state in life and recite daily her Little Office or fulfill an approved Marian practice will be released from Purgatory the first Saturday after their death. The Brown Scapular is blessed with many indulgences and is a sign that we belong to Mary who is perfectly consecrated to the will of God. She is prefigured on Mount Carmel by the cloud which poured forth a bountiful rain, a sign of sanctifying grace that would descend to earth in the incarnation of Eternal Wisdom. She is the garden and vine of God through which God fulfills His covenant with man that was renewed on Mount Carmel after Elijah converted the prophets of Baal to belief in the one true God with fire from heaven. Mary is an icon of divine grace, *gratia plena*, that brings forth Divine Wisdom, the new mountain of contemplation. At Fátima in 1917, she appeared as Our Lady of Mount Carmel in the miracle of the sun, confirming devotion to the Brown Scapular that clothes us with her virtues. She is the spiritual mother of mankind who forms the life of Jesus in us that we may love God as she loves Him in her Immaculate Heart.

Prayer to Our Lady of Mount Carmel

O most blessed and immaculate Virgin, ornament and beauty of Mount Carmel, thou who beholdest with thy special kindness those who wear thy blessed Scapular, look lovingly upon me, and cover me with the mantle of thy motherly protection. Fortify my weakness with thy power, enlighten the darkness of my understanding with thy wisdom, increase Faith, Hope and Charity in me, adorn my soul with the graces and virtues that will make me pleasing to thee and thy divine Son. Assist me during my life, and console me at the hour of my death and present me to the most blessed Trinity as thy devoted servant, to praise and bless thee in heaven forever. Amen.

St. Catherine Labouré

CATHERINE LABOURÉ was born in Fain-les-Moutiers, France in 1806. When she was young, her mother died and she cared for the family without attending school. She desired to become a nun to serve the elderly and the sick. In 1830 she entered the Daughters of Charity founded by St. Vincent de Paul. That same year, her guardian angel led her to the convent chapel for the first of three apparitions of Our Lady. On the third visit, Our Lady told her to have a medal made in honor of the Immaculate Conception with the words "O Mary, conceived without sin, pray for us who have recourse to thee" on the frontside and an image of Hearts of Jesus and Mary on the back. In 1832, the Archbishop of Paris permitted the making of the medal and in 1836 he approved the apparitions. The medal, known as the Miraculous Medal, spread throughout the world and became instrumental in obtaining cures, conversions and graces for "persons who wear it with confidence." Until her death in 1876, St. Catherine did not reveal her visions to anyone except her confessor and continued to serve the infirm in a hospice. She was canonized in 1947 and her body has remained incorrupt. The devotion of the Miraculous Medal is extensively promoted by members of the Legion of Mary.

The Miraculous Medal

O Lord Jesus Christ, Who preserved Thy Mother, the Blessed Virgin Mary free from the stain of sin at the moment of her conception and was pleased that she should shine with countless miracles of grace, grant that through her patronage we may obtain the joy of everlasting life. Amen.

St. Catherine Labouré

Lord our God, Who granted unto St. Catherine a vision of the Immaculate Virgin Mary, Thy Mother, we ask Thee after the example of blessed Catherine for a tender devotion to Thy holy Mother that we may enjoy the grace of eternal life. Amen.

St. Catherine of Siena; St. Rose

CATHERINE BENINCASA was born in Siena, Italy in 1347, the youngest of twenty-five children in her family. At age six, she received a vision of Jesus. After she became a third order Dominican at age eighteen, she lived at home and for three years spoke only to God and her confessor. She converted sinners, nursed the sick and worked miracles for the poor. When she fasted, her only food was Holy Communion. She supported the Crusades and convinced the pope to return the papal throne to Rome. She wrote a book, the *Dialogue*, about her mystical experiences and received the invisible stigmata in 1375. She died in 1380, was canonized in 1461 and became a Doctor of the Church in 1970. St. Rose, born in 1586 in Lima, Peru, was named Rose after her mother saw a rose drooping over her crib. She became a third order Dominican, received the invisible stigmata and was devoted to the Passion of Christ, praying and sacrificing for sinners. She lived in a small hut in her father's garden where Jesus appeared to her. Her head was crowned with thorns over which she wore a crown of roses. She died in 1617 and was canonized the first American saint in 1671.

St. Catherine of Siena

Most Holy Spirit, source of unity in the Blessed Trinity, through the prayers of St. Catherine, may the Church always be a sign of unity in faith and morals under the leadership of the Holy Father, the divinely chosen authority who speaks in the name of Jesus Christ. Who with the Father and the Son lives and reigns forever. Amen.

St. Rose of Lima

Almighty God, Who bestows bountiful gifts, and willed that St. Rose, bedewed with heavenly gifts, should blossom forth as a lovely flower of virginity and patience, may we follow her way and become a sweet savor of Christ. We ask this through Christ our Lord. Amen.

St. Charles Borromeo; St. Aloysius

CHARLES BORROMEO was born in a castle in Arona, Italy in 1538. He studied at an abbey and received a doctorate in canon law in 1552. His uncle, Pope Pius IV, made him the cardinal and archbishop of Milan at age twenty-two. He was ordained and made a bishop in 1563. He established schools, hospitals, seminaries, a community of oblates for the sanctity of priests and a religious education program for youth. As bishop, he held over ten synods, organized relief efforts to alleviate famine and plague and personally fed 3,000 famine victims daily for three months. A major figure in the Counter Reformation, he implemented the teachings of the Council of Trent on doctrine and the liturgy and participated in writing the Roman Catechism. His catechetical teachings and pastoral visitations brought many Catholics back to the Church. He died in 1584 and was canonized in 1610. St. Aloysius Gonzaga, born in 1568 in Lombardy, Italy received his First Holy Communion from St. Charles. A royal page, he aspired to the religious life and joined the Jesuits in 1585. He was a model of purity known for his heroic charity and penance. He died from a plague in 1591 while caring for plague victims in Rome. He was canonized in 1726 and is the patron of Catholic youth.

St. Charles Borromeo

O Lord, may the pastoral zeal of Thy Confessor and Bishop, St. Charles, set before the Church the example of a faithful shepherd whose love for the Church and wealth of teaching guides the flock of Christ to the glory of eternal life. Amen.

St. Aloysius Gonzaga

O God, grant that, through the merits and prayers of St. Aloysius, we may follow his angelic life of innocence and his spirit of penance and come to the heavenly banquet to dwell in Thy courts forever. Amen.

The Child Jesus

THE CHILD JESUS, Who was born of the House of David, is both God and Man, the Son of the eternal Father, and the Son of the Virgin Mary. He assumed human nature to become the Lamb of God to take away the sins of the world and to be the author of the generation and restoration of divine life in souls. He teaches us to become a child of God the Father, to live for God, to obey His divine law and to preserve the grace of innocence in renouncing the deceptions of the world, the flesh and the devil. In His Heart are found all the treasures of wisdom and understanding. The Child Jesus was seen in the miracle of the sun at Fátima on Oct. 13, 1917. He and His Mother on Dec. 10, 1925 told Sr. Lucy, the surviving seer of the Fátima visions, to console the Heart of Mary through the devotion of five consecutive First Saturdays. On Feb. 15, 1926, the Child Jesus said He was pleased with those who make reparation to the Immaculate Heart of Mary. Through His incarnation and birth, the Child Jesus, God the Son made man, is the light of God's salvation shining upon all mankind.

Prayer to the Child Jesus

O most holy Child Jesus, I know You love me and come near me to make me a child of God. You are my teacher and savior who never leaves me and always gives me hope. I believe You are the Prince of Peace and I learn from You to treasure the sacred gift of childhood as a sign of my eternal destiny in heaven in union with Your Father. Lord Jesus, may I love You more. Amen.

The Divine Child

A Child is born to us, a Son is given to us and upon His shoulders kingship rests. The Lord has made known His salvation through the Divine Child of the Virgin Mary's womb that reveals His justice in the sight of the nations. Our God and Savior, Jesus Christ, became a Child that He might cleanse for Himself an acceptable people. Amen.

Christic the King

CHRIST THE KING is a feast day solemnly instituted in 1925 by Pope Pius XI to proclaim the complete dominion and social reign of Jesus Christ over individuals, families, nations and the world. Christ is the "King and center of all hearts," arrayed in the splendor of the Father, Who subjects the conscience, mind and will of man to divine law to counteract secularism that organizes society as if God did not exist. As the sovereign Lord of creation and Eternal Priest Who overcomes the slavery of sin and death, His royalty is universal. His rule is observed by Christian kings and rulers who uphold the supernatural rights of God and the Church in society. He is the "lion of the tribe of Judah, the Root of David," Who establishes an eternal kingdom, that is not of this world, through the Blood of His cross, His royal scepter of power. Born to "rule over the house of Jacob," Christ sacrifices Himself to give testimony to the truth of the kingdom of God and win the crown of everlasting life. He will come again to judge the world as King of kings and Lord of lords, the great King above all gods. Through Him, the faithful win a glorious victory over the powers of hell and, in the regal splendor of His heavenly court, worship before the throne of His Sacred Heart.

Christ the King

Almighty and eternal God, Who through Thy beloved Son, the sovereign King of the whole world, has willed to restore all things in Him, mercifully grant that all the nations that are divided by sin may be brought to unity under the dominion of His loving rule. Who lives and reigns with the Father and the Holy Spirit, for ever and ever. Amen.

The Lamb Once Slain

The Lamb that was slain is worthy to receive power and divinity and wisdom and strength and honor; to Him be glory and riches for ever and ever. Give to the King, O God, Thy justice and to the King's Son Thy judgment. Amen.

Et Ipse est ante omnia

St. Clare of Assisi

CLARE was born in 1194 in Assisi, Italy. She was the daughter of a noble, and at age eighteen was inspired by a sermon of St. Francis to leave all things for Christ and embrace holy poverty. She accepted a penitential habit from St. Francis, and despite family opposition, remained resolute in her vocation. In 1215, Clare moved to a house near the San Damiano church and founded the order of the Poor Clares, where her widowed mother and two of her sisters joined the community. Members of her order were to mortify themselves by walking barefoot, sleeping on the ground and always abstaining from meat. Clare was visited by many bishops and popes during the forty years she was abbess, and she firmly insisted on the absolute renunciation of property in her rule of life. During an attempted siege of her convent, she repelled an invading army by holding the Blessed Sacrament at the convent gate. Clare was a translucent example of Franciscan spirituality in her love for holy poverty and in the contemplation of Christ, Who "will keep your virginity ever unspotted." She died in 1253 and was canonized in 1255. Clare believed that "he who loves temporal things loses the fruit of love." The observance of the penitential practices of the Poor Clares have made them powerful intercessors before God.

St. Clare, Virgin

God our Father, You chose the consecrated soul of St. Clare as a victim of expiation and praise in Your Son's great work of Redemption. May we follow her in the spirit of holy poverty and come to the vision of Your eternal glory. Through Christ our Lord. Amen.

Prayer to St. Clare

Dear St. Clare, wise and prudent virgin, help us to make good use of our time to know and do the holy will of God, that we may refrain from the excessive use of television and live morally upright lives in the service of God's truth. We ask this through Christ our Lord. Amen.

David and Goliath

DAVID, the youngest of the eight sons of Jesse of Bethlehem, was a charming, young shepherd whom the prophet Samuel anointed to be the future King of Israel. He was an excellent harpist and speaker and the spirit of the Lord was upon him. In a battle between the Israelites and the Philistines, a giant named Goliath challenged the Israelites to send one man into battle with him to determine which side would be the victor. While on an errand to bring food to three of his brothers in the battle, David heard Goliath's challenge and his insults against the armies of the Lord. With his faith in the living God, David volunteered to avenge the insults and to fight the giant the way he slew wild animals. He set aside the armor that was too hard to wear and went into battle with a staff, a sling and five round stones from the wadi in his shepherd's bag. He declared, in the name of the Lord, that he would strike Goliath down. David flung a single stone with his sling that struck Goliath dead in the forehead and then cut off the giant's head. God was glorified through David's staff and sling which prefigures Christ's cross that defeats the "prince of this world," and Mary's Rosary that can crush the head of Satan with a single Hail Mary.

The Lord is God

Lord, You have been our refuge from generation unto generation. Before the mountains were made or the earth and the world was formed, You are God from eternity to eternity. I have hoped in Your word to execute judgment on the wicked. Help me, O Lord, my God. Amen. Alleluia.

Bless the Lord

Bless the Lord, O my soul, and never forget all His benefits. May my youth be renewed like that of an eagle. Let my heart rejoice to seek the Lord and be strengthened to seek His face evermore. Give glory to the Lord and call upon His Name that His justice be proclaimed. Amen.

Jesus, Mary, Joseph assist me in my last agony!

The Death of Joseph

ST. JOSEPH, the spouse of the Virgin Mary and the foster father of Jesus, God the Son made man, is the last of the patriarchs to lead, guide and protect the covenant of God that is fulfilled in Jesus. Joseph was not the New Adam, but at the message of an angel, he became the guardian of the mystery of the incarnation of Life itself. He anticipated the sufferings of Jesus in the prophecy of Simeon and, like Moses, delivered the family of God out of its exile in Egypt to the promised land and was privileged to behold the face of God. He was the father of the hidden life of Jesus until His public ministry began when the Father proclaimed Him "My Son." Joseph was a just man favored by God who lived and died in the presence of God and the Mother of God. He surrendered himself at death into the hands of Jesus and Mary in gratitude and in joy to God Who entrusted him with the care of His Son. After death, he entered the abode of the just and confidently awaited deliverance into the promised land of heaven that came through the resurrection of Jesus. Joseph is the patron of a happy death and of the Universal Church who safely leads the children of God through the valley of darkness to the eternal home of heaven.

Prayer for a Happy Death

O my Lord and Savior, support me in my last hour by the strong arms of Thy sacraments and the fragrance of Thy consolations. Let Thy absolving words be said over me and the holy oil sign and seal me. Let Thine own Body be my food and Thy Blood my sprinkling and let Thy Mother Mary come to me and my angel whisper peace to me and Thy glorious saints and my own dear patrons smile on me, that in and through them all I may die as I desire to live, in Thy Church, in Thy faith and in Thy love. Amen.

St. Dominic

S T. DOMINIC was born in Calaruega, Spain in 1170. He was the son of a knight, and his greatness was foretold in the vision of a running dog lighting up the world with a torch and by a star seen above his forehead at baptism. At age seven, Dominic was schooled in the classics in a town that was on the road that led to the shrine of St. James at Compostela. He devoted himself to prayer and study during his university years, and sold some of his books to help feed the poor. At twenty-five, he entered the religious life and was ordained in 1195. He travelled with a bishop in 1203 to preach against the Albigensian heresy, and later founded an order of preachers which combined penance, prayer and study for the purpose of saving souls through the preaching and teaching of God's word. According to tradition, the Blessed Virgin told him to preach the devotion of the Holy Rosary, "the psalter of the lay people," as an effective weapon against heresy. His order included friars and nuns, and was approved by Pope Honorius III. Many converted to the Catholic faith through his preaching and his miraculous power. He once blessed a well which restored health to the sick that drank from it. He died in 1221 and was canonized in 1234. In the first hundred years of the Dominican order, 13,000 members were martyred.

St. Dominic, Confessor

O God, through the merits and teaching of St. Dominic, Your devoted Confessor, Your Church was gloriously acclaimed. Grant that, through his intercession, she may always advance in her spiritual and temporal mission of salvation. Through Christ our Lord. Amen.

Prayer to St. Dominic

O most holy priest of God, St. Dominic, you are the beloved son of the Queen of heaven who worked many miracles. Intercede for my needs before the Mother of the most Holy Rosary and her eternal Son that I may obtain the favor I ask. Amen.

The Four Evangelists

THE EVANGELISTS MATTHEW, MARK, LUKE AND JOHN, symbolized by a man, a lion, an ox and an eagle, are the four inspired Gospel writers that proclaim the "Good News" of Jesus Christ. Matthew traces the origin of Jesus from Abraham to Joseph and says that the kingdom of heaven begins with Jesus and is definitively fulfilled in His Second Coming at the end of time. The community of believers in Jesus forms the Church which is built on the Apostle Peter. Mark wrote his Gospel from the teachings of St. Peter in which Jesus, the Son of God, is enthroned as King of the world on Calvary and is vindicated in His resurrection. Luke shows the compassion and mercy of Jesus and that salvation is possible for anyone who believes in Jesus. Man's union with God begins with the incarnation of Jesus and is continued through grace and prayer. John declares that Jesus is the eternal Word made flesh, the Lamb of God, Who is the "I am" of salvation that reveals the Father. He is the temple of God and the revelation of Truth that grants eternal life through the gift of the Holy Spirit. The Church has the mission to teach about the commands, miracles and parables of Jesus and to preach His Gospel to the ends of the earth.

The Four Gospels

O God, may the inspired writing of the Gospels increase love for Thy Word and fidelity to Thy commands through the teaching authority of the Church that her mission of preaching the divine revelation of Jesus will reveal His life in the world. Through Christ Jesus, Who is Lord for ever and ever. Amen.

The Light of Salvation

The heavens declare Thy wonders, O Lord. May Thy Name be great among the nations that all people will praise Thee. May Thy salvation be known upon the earth for there is no one beside Thee. Thy truth endures forever and Thy light shines upon the earth through Thy servants. Praise the God of our salvation.

The Message of Fátima

SISTER LUCY DOS SANTOS, born in 1907, is the living witness of the six apparitions approved by the Church of Our Lady of the Rosary at Fátima, Portugal from May to October 1917. She was one of three children to whom Our Lady appeared and delivered an apocalyptic message of the annihilation of nations that could be prevented through a daily Rosary, penance and the consecration of Russia to her Immaculate Heart. Our Lady said God wished to establish in the world devotion to her Immaculate Heart to lead souls to heaven, to convert sinners, to make Communions of reparation on the First Saturdays of the month and to bring about a period of peace in the world and the conversion of Russia. Her message was confirmed on Oct.13 by the many conversions that resulted from a miracle in which the sun fell from its orbit but resumed its normal course before engulfing the earth in fire. Through the Heart of Mary, God transmits the grace of salvation and in her Heart dwells Jesus, the peace and salvation of the world. Her Heart is a refuge for souls and the prophesied triumph of her Immaculate Heart will be a supernatural assent to the truths of the Catholic faith.

Consecration to the Immaculate Heart of Mary

O Immaculate Heart of Mary, refuge of sinners and comfort of the afflicted, I consecrate myself to thee and offer thee a daily Rosary along with my sacrifices for the conversion of sinners. I promise to be faithful to my baptismal promises, to renounce the devil and to receive Holy Communion on the First Saturdays of the month in reparation for the sins committed against thee and thy Son. May thy Immaculate Heart reign over me and make my heart like thine where the Heart of thy Son reigned and triumphed. In thy Heart, O Mary, full of grace, dwells the triumph of the kingdom of God in the world. May my consecration to thy Immaculate Heart hasten the day of peace on earth that all people will bless thee and praise the glorious victory of the Heart of Jesus. Amen.

Blessed Sr. Faustina, pray for us!

JESUS, I TRUST IN YOU!

Blessed Faustina Kowalska

BLESSED SISTER MARY FAUSTINA KOWALSKA was born on Aug. 25, 1905 in the small village of Glogowiec, Poland. Her baptismal name was Helen, and at the age of seven she heard God calling her to the religious life. At eighteen, she asked her parents for permission to enter a convent, but they refused. She remained in the world, trying to understand God's call. Then she heard a voice calling her to Warsaw, where, on Aug. 1, 1925, she became a postulant in the Congregation of the Sisters of Our Lady of Mercy and made her perpetual vows on May 1, 1933. During her convent life, she did baking, gardening and was a gatekeeper, and experienced much physical and spiritual suffering. She received many spiritual communications from Jesus Who asked her to spread devotion to The Divine Mercy, especially through a chaplet and a painting. She died in Cracow on Oct. 5, 1938 and was beatified on Mercy Sunday, Apr. 18, 1993 by Pope John Paul II who began the Informative Process for her cause while he was Archbishop of Cracow.

Prayer for Mercy

O Jesus, font of Mercy, ever flowing from Your Sacred Heart, Your Divine Heart is Mercy itself. May I know the depth of Your merciful love, which has redeemed the world. Your mercy is my sanctity and salvation that gives You great glory. You, O Divine Jesus, are the delight and joy of my whole being. Have mercy on me, for I have sinned in Your sight. With the help of Your grace and the prayers of Blessed Sr. Faustina, I will worship Your Divine Mercy, and patiently submit to Your divine will, which is nourishment for my soul. Glory, praise and honor to The Divine Mercy of Jesus, now and forever. Amen.

St. Francis de Sales; St. Jane

S T. FRANCIS DE SALES was born near Annecy, France in 1567. He earned a doctorate in civil law, but abandoned a secular career to become a priest in 1593. He began a five year mission to the Calvinists that won him thousands of converts. In 1599, he was made co-adjutor bishop of Geneva and succeeded to the see in 1602. He established a seminary and instructed his priests to preach and teach the faith in simple language. A man of great meekness and modesty, Francis taught that holiness is possible in any state of life and he published many ascetical writings, among them his spiritual classics *The Introduction to the Devout Life* and *The Treatise on Divine Love*. He died in 1622, was canonized in 1665 and declared a Doctor of the Church in 1877. St. Jane Frances de Chantal was born in Dijon, France in 1572. She was married in 1592, raised seven children and was happily married for eight years. After her husband died, she met St. Francis de Sales, a spiritual friend, and after making suitable provisions for her children, followed his direction in founding the order of the Visitation. Sixty convents were established during her lifetime. She died in 1641 and was canonized in 1767.

St. Francis de Sales

O God, by Thy will, St. Francis de Sales, Confessor and Bishop, was all things to all men for the salvation of souls, grant that, being filled with Thy love, we may follow his counsels and benefit from the merits of his gentle wisdom to inherit the grace of everlasting life. Through Christ our Lord. Amen.

St. Jane de Chantal

Enkindle in us, O Lord, that divine fire of the Holy Spirit which consumed the soul of Francis de Sales and enlightened the heart of St. Jane Frances de Chantal that the grace of Thy incarnation may be welcomed in the hearts of all mankind. We ask this through Christ our Lord. Amen.

Blessed Gianna Beretta Molla

BLESSED GIANNA BERETTA MOLLA, a pediatrician from Milan and mother of three children, at the age of thirty-nine, decided to carry her fourth child to term rather than undergo the removal of a tumor that would have required the abortion of her child. Seven days after she gave birth to a girl named Gianna Emanuela, who is still living today, Gianna Molla died on Apr. 28, 1962. She sacrificed her life to give birth to her unborn child and acted as a mother, doing everything to save her child. In union with the sacrifice of Jesus, her love for life was faithful unto death. She accepted the child as a gift of God and would not let inconvenience abort her child's right to life. In light of her generosity, her life-giving charity transcends the social forces of vanity and brings forth a ray of light into a prevailing culture of death. In Gianna, gratitude is given to God for the gift of the child and life is given that another may live. She is a heroic model of fidelity to the dignity and vocation of a woman as wife and mother. She was beatified by Pope John Paul II in May 1993.

Prayer for Childbirth

Heavenly Father, Creator of human life, may the example and prayers of Blessed Gianna, who sacrificed her life to give life to her innocent unborn child and who chose to bring her child to term out of her love for Your gift of the child as well as the child's right to be born and baptized into Your kingdom, inspire mothers with difficult pregnancies to have the courage to bring their children to term and after birth to give them the love they deserve. Through Christ our Lord. Amen.

The Good Shepherd

THE GOOD SHEPHERD is Jesus, the only Son of God Who became man, and laid down His life to gather the sheep straying in the bondage of sin into the one sheepfold of His Church founded on the rock of the Apostle Peter. Jesus knows and loves His sheep and they know and love Him. He feeds them with the gift and grace of His eternal life, His own Sacred Body and Most Precious Blood in the Holy Eucharist. He guides His flock through the teaching authority of His Church, where the sheep hear and follow His voice, the voice of the Shepherd and guardian of their souls, because "I know mine and mine know Me." He is the Shepherd Who laid down His life to redeem one flock, and apart from His rule the sheep can not be saved. He enfolds His sheep in the arms of His gentle, loving care, and they trust that His staff will protect them from evil. The Good Shepherd leads His sheep through the valleys and hills of life to His eternal pasture, where they will wear white robes washed in "the blood of the Lamb." The Good Shepherd is the Lamb of salvation Who leads His flock to the springs of everlasting life flowing from His Most Sacred Heart.

The Good Shepherd

The Lord is my Shepherd; there is nothing I shall want. He gives me rest in fresh green pastures. He leads me near restful waters to restore my drooping spirit. He guides me along right paths; He is true to His word. If I should walk in the shadow of darkness, no evil shall I fear. You are there with the strength of Your staff, which gives me Your comfort. You have served me a banquet in the presence of my foes. You have anointed my head with oil; my cup overflows. Surely goodness and kindness will follow me everyday of my life. In the Lord's own temple I will dwell, for ever and ever.

St. Hermenegild

Martyr of the Eucharist

St. Hermenegild

ST. HERMENEGILD was born the son of Leovigild, an Arian King of Spain. His father made him a prince of his Visigothic kingdom in Seville, and he married a devout Catholic, the daughter of the King of Austrasia in France. Through her example and the teaching of St. Leander, Archbishop of Seville, he was converted from his Arianism to the Catholic faith. His father, upon hearing of his son's new found faith, decided to take away his duties and possessions, and even his life if he refused to return to Arian beliefs. But he refused, and his father had him put in prison, charging him with the offense of heresy. During Eastertime in 586, he sent an Arian bishop to his son, hoping to win his favor if he would receive Holy Communion from the bishop. Hermenegild declined, and his father, in a burst of anger, had the young prince put to death. St. Hermenegild died a martyr of the Holy Eucharist rather than renounce his Catholic faith in the consubstantiality of the Word of God. St. Gregory the Great credits him with the conversion of Visigothic Spain and his brother, Reccared, a son of Leovigild. His feast day is Apr. 13.

St. Hermenegild, Martyr

O God, Who inspired blessed Hermenegild, Thy martyr, to choose the Kingdom of Heaven rather than an earthy throne, grant us, we beseech Thee, that, following his example, we may despise the fleeting things of the world and of time and follow after those that are eternal. We ask this through our Lord Jesus Christ, Thy Son, Who lives and reigns with Thee in the unity of the Holy Spirit, one God, for ever and ever. Amen.

Lord of Life

"I am the Resurrection"

"**I** AM THE RESURRECTION AND THE LIFE," Jesus says. He is the Lord of Life, the fullness of life and existence itself, Who rose from the dead on the third day *"sicut dixit,"* and to Whom is due the homage of "my Lord and my God." The resurrection of Jesus Christ from the dead is not a return to a previously lived life or a miraculous resuscitation. It is the beginning of a new life for man in which the Risen Christ enters His glory at the right hand of the Father. The resurrection is a doctrine of faith necessary for salvation and without which the Church's faith is meaningless. In His resurrection from the dead, the Crucified and Risen Christ appears to His disciples who touch, speak and eat with Him. His resurrection anticipates the resurrection of the dead at the end of the world, when those who are worthy of Christ and His love will rise to an eternal communion of love and life in Him. They will be reconstituted in a glorified body not subject to the limitations of an earthly or cosmic existence. They will be under the rule of the Holy Spirit Who glorifies the victory of "the Lamb once slain." The resurrection of Jesus Christ from the dead frees mankind from the slavery of sin and death and promises the grace of eternal life to those who live for Him.

The Glory of the Lord

O God, Who illumines the world by the glory of the Lord's Resurrection, preserve in the new children of Thy family the spirit of adoption which Thou hast given, that renewed in body and mind, they may render to Thee a pure and fitting service. Through Jesus Christ our Lord Who lives for ever and ever. Amen.

The Eternal Gate

O God, Who through Thine only-begotten Son, has conquered sin and death and opened the gates of everlasting life, grant that Thy servants may always adhere to the glorious mystery of the Lord's Resurrection which they have received by faith. We ask this through Christ our Lord. Amen.

Blessed Imelda

IMELDA was born to a wealthy family in Bologna, Italy in 1322. On her fifth birthday, she told her parents of her desire to receive Holy Communion even though fourteen was the required age. She committed herself to the study of the Catholic faith and decided to become a Dominican nun. At the age of nine, she was admitted to a Dominican convent and frequently prayed for Jesus to come and dwell in her soul. One day in 1333, while kneeling in the convent chapel, a consecrated Host appeared in a splendid light over the altar and going forth came to rest above Imelda's head, where she gazed upon It in ecstasy. She remained kneeling for a long time, desiring to receive Jesus in Holy Communion. A priest was summoned to give Imelda the Host. She received the Host and continued to kneel for a very long time, prompting the Mother Superior to determine the reason why. She found that Imelda had died. Out of her great love for Jesus, she died after receiving her First Holy Communion. Imelda was beatified by Pope Leo XII in 1826 and is the patroness of First Holy Communicants.

After Holy Communion

Jesus, You are my Lord and my God. I thank You for coming to visit me in the real presence of Your Body, Blood, Soul and Divinity. I ask, through the prayers of Blessed Imelda, that You will reign over my heart and never let me be separated from You. May I serve You faithfully that I may adore and glorify You forever in heaven. Amen.

Prayer of Thanksgiving

Dear Jesus, I thank Thee for nourishing me with Thy Sacred Body and Most Precious Blood. I am grateful for the blessings I have received through the merits of Thy Passion applied to my soul in the Holy Sacrifice of the Mass. May my devotion to Thee in this sacrament of Thy love make me adhere to Thy will and become more like Thee. Amen.

St. Jerome

JEROME was born in 342 in the small Dalmatian town of Stridon. His father taught him the ways of piety, and then sent him to Rome for study, where he mastered the classical languages of Latin and Greek, and became an orator. He was baptized, and then travelled with friends to further his studies. He spent four years in a Syrian desert in prayer and study with the virtuous Abbot Theodosius, and learned to overcome temptations of the flesh. While in Antioch in 377, he was ordained a priest. He studied the scriptures under St. Gregory Nazianzen in Constantinople, and then attended a council in Rome called by Pope St. Damascus, who later made him his secretary. Jerome wrote a book defending the perpetual virginity of Mary. In 385, he set sail for the Holy Land, and lived in a cave-like cell near the birthplace of Jesus, studying Sacred Scripture and directing a monastery in Bethlehem founded by St. Paula. St. Jerome is a Father and Doctor of the Church, renowned for his translation of Sacred Scripture into Latin, the *Vulgate* version approved by Pope St. Gregory the Great. He died in Bethlehem on Sept. 30, 420, and is the patron of librarians.

St. Jerome, Doctor of the Church

O God, Who in holy and blessed Jerome, Thy Confessor, did provide for Thy Church a great and venerable teacher for expounding the truth of Sacred Scripture, grant we beseech Thee, that through his merits and prayers we may be able, by the help of Thy grace, to practice what he taught by word and example. Through Christ our Lord. Amen.

Jesus is Laid in the Tomb

AFTER Jesus was taken down from the Cross and placed in the arms of His Mother, Joseph of Arimathea and Nicodemus brought the linen and spices for the burial of Jesus. They wrapped His body in the linen along with the spices and carried Him to Joseph's new tomb that was hewn out in a rock. Mary, the Mother of Jesus, Mary Magdalen and some of the holy women of Jerusalem accompanied them. According to tradition, the apostle John was joined in the procession to the tomb by the apostles Peter and James, and along the way, all creation mourned the death of Him through Whom all things were made. The trees and flowers bent in homage, the birds sang a melancholy song, the ground trembled, the sun dimmed its light and the angels bowed in adoration. The Passion of Jesus began and ended in a garden. He was the seed of eternal life placed in a sepulcher from which death would die through His resurrection from the dead. Our hearts must be the new resting place for the Risen Body of Christ in Holy Communion, an abode uncontaminated by the world that we must guard with the immutable truth of Christ and the fragrant grace of Christian virtue.

The Passion of Jesus

O God, Who left us a record of Thy Passion in the holy shroud, wherein Joseph wrapped Thy Sacred Body when taken down from the Cross, mercifully grant that through Thy death and burial we may be brought to the glory of Thy resurrection. Through Christ our Lord. Amen.

The Good Sower

O God, Who by the voice of the holy Prophets has declared to all the children of Thy Church that Thou art the Sower of good seed and the Cultivator of chosen branches, grant to Thy people who are Thy vine and harvestfield, that they may root out all thorns and briars and produce good fruit in abundance. We ask this through Christ our Lord. Amen.

St. Joan of Arc

JOAN OF ARC, *Jeanne-la-Puelle*, a consecrated daughter of God, was born in Domrémy, France on Jan. 6, 1412. She was a shepherd girl, the youngest of five children of Jacques D'arc. Joan was a chaste, reverent, gentle, yet courageous Christian who, at a young age, heard the heavenly Voices of saints calling her to receive the sacraments frequently and to undertake the liberation of France from the occupation of the British. Convinced of her heavenly mission, she sought permission from the exiled King of France to begin her military campaign. He agreed, and she rode into battle dressed in white armor, riding a horse and bearing a banner that read "Jesus, Mary" and "In the Name of the King of Heaven." Her army won impressive victories, most notably at Orleans, which resulted in the restoration of the King who was crowned at Rheims on July 17, 1429. Joan lost a battle in Paris and then was captured by the British. She was tried by a Church court where many testified against the credibility of her mission and her Catholic faith. She was falsely condemned as a heretic and delivered to the civil authorities who had her burned with fire on May 30, 1431. The Church re-opened her case in 1456 and found her innocent. She was canonized in 1920 and is a patroness of France.

St. Joan of Arc, Virgin

Lord our God, You have blessed us with the heroic life of Joan, Your holy Virgin, to defend the Catholic faith and her country from the snares of her enemies. Grant that, through her intercession, Your Church may enjoy the peace and unity it signifies. We ask this through Christ our Lord. Amen.

St. John the Baptist

JOHN THE BAPTIST, the forerunner and precursor of Jesus Christ, was the son of Zachary, a Jewish priest, and Elizabeth, a cousin of the Virgin Mary, and was born in Ain-Karim six months before Jesus. As an unborn child, "filled with the Holy Spirit from his mother's womb," John leapt for joy upon seeing Jesus in the womb of Mary when she came to visit Elizabeth. At that moment, he was pre-sanctified, and was born without Original Sin, a birthday celebrated in the Church since the 4th century. His name and birth was revealed by the angel Gabriel, and in thanksgiving his father uttered the *Benedictus*. John was consecrated to the Lord from birth. He lived in solitude in a desert in Judea, where he wore penitential garments, and at age twenty-seven began preaching a baptism of repentance at the Jordan river. He spoke in the spirit and power of Elijah, "for the kingdom of God is at hand." When he baptized Jesus, heralding Him as "the Lamb of God Who takes away the sin of the world," the heavens opened, a dove descended and the Father said "this is My Son." Jesus declared that there is "no greater prophet born of woman" than John. He was martyred by King Herod, and was the last of the great prophets, a fearless teacher and a virgin, who was commissioned to inaugurate the coming of God's kingdom.

St. John the Baptist, Martyr

May Thy holy Church, O Lord, rejoice at the birth of John the Baptist who prepared the way for Jesus, the Author of salvation, and through his prayers, may she always courageously teach that the unborn child is the fruit of true love. We ask this through Christ our Lord. Amen.

The Herald of God

O St. John the Baptist, undefiled herald proclaiming the reign of God's kingdom, help us to be faithful to our promises of baptism in rejecting the world, the flesh and the devil, that we may follow the teaching of Jesus that leads to eternal life. This we ask through Christ our Lord. Amen.

St. John Neumann

JOHN NEPOMUCENE NEUMANN, the "sturdy mountain boy," was born Mar. 28, 1811 in Prachatiz, Bohemia. He was drawn to the religious life and entered a seminary in Prague, but could not be ordained due to an overabundance of priests in Bohemia. In 1836, he came to the Unites States and was ordained in New York. He spent much time in mission work among German Catholics. He joined the Redemptorists in 1840 and became the American superior in 1847. He was named the fourth bishop of Philadelphia in 1852 and built many churches, schools, established a seminary and founded an order of sisters of St. Francis. He was the first to publish the *Kyriale* in the United States and wrote two catechisms approved by the American bishops that were extensively used in Catholic schools. In his diocese, vespers was sung in the churches on Sunday, the clergy attended an annual retreat, and in 1853 Forty Hours devotion began among the parishes. Bishop Neumann believed in personally bringing Christ to his flock through frequent pastoral visits. He died in 1860 and was canonized June 19, 1977. His motto was "Passion of Christ, strengthen me."

Bishop St. John Neumann

God our Father, may the goodness, generosity, charity and sacrifice exemplified in the life of Bishop Neumann encourage all bishops to a life of dedication, zeal and fidelity to Thy Son, Jesus Christ, and His Church. We ask this through Jesus Christ our Lord. Amen.

Prayer for Holiness

Lord Jesus Christ, may the worship of Thy divine mysteries lead the faithful to a greater holiness of life and a deeper understanding of Thy teachings for which St. John Neumann labored to bring honor and glory to Thy Name. Amen.

Blessed Juan Diego

JUAN DIEGO, born in 1474 near Mexico City with the name Cuauhtlatohuac meaning "the eagle who speaks," was baptized in 1525 along with his wife and uncle. On his way to morning Mass on Dec. 9, 1531, the Spanish feast of the Immaculate Conception, Juan heard music from Tepeyac hill and saw a beautiful lady standing before a bright white cloud who said, "I am truly the perpetual and perfect Virgin Mary, holy mother of the true God through whom everything lives." She told Juan to ask the bishop to build a church on the hill. The bishop said that he needed a sign, and on Dec. 12 Our Lady told Juan to gather the flowers blooming on the hillside into his tilma, and after she arranged them, to show them to the bishop. When Juan opened his tilma, the bishop saw red roses fall to the floor and beheld a miraculous portrait of Our Lady on the tilma. He gave permission to build a chapel and Juan became the guardian of the heavenly treasure and the evangelizer of millions of Aztecs who were converted to the Catholic faith. The holy image, known as Our Lady of Guadalupe, was a sign that she who crushes the stone serpent and overcomes the mother-goddess with the purity of her faith, will gather into the mantle of her heavenly protection the fragrant flowers of faith in her Son. Juan died in 1548 and was beatified May 6, 1990.

Mother of the True God

Most Holy Mary, ever Virgin and Mother of the living and true God Who became man for our salvation, may the Church, built on the faith of Peter, become a flower garden of sanctity through the prayers of Blessed Juan Diego, your spiritual son, where new flowers of divine faith will be planted to glorify Your Son and honor you as the mother of mankind. Amen.

King David

DAVID, the youngest son of Jesse, was born in Bethlehem around 1040 B.C. He was a shepherd who killed a bear and a lion to protect his father's flock. As a youth, he was anointed by the prophet Samuel to be the future King of Israel. An occasional harpist and servant for King Saul, David became famous when he stood alone to defend the fortunes of Israel and killed a Philistine giant named Goliath. David entered the king's service and became a warrior and his power and fame grew as he won impressive military battles. King Saul became envious and sought to destroy David. But David escaped and after Saul was killed in a battle, he established his throne in Hebron and then in Jerusalem as the King of Israel. He built a tabernacle for the Ark of the Covenant and made plans to build a temple for the worship of God. Although David ruled with great equity and justice, favored by God as "a man after my own heart," he was chastised by the prophet Nathan for committing adultery and repented. David reigned as king for forty years and died in 970 B.C. He was the "sweet psalmist of Israel," and the ancestor of Jesus Christ, the root of Jesse, Who was born of the House of David in Bethlehem and Whose kingdom has no end.

The Reign of God

O God, You have made known Your salvation in the sight of the nations. Your anointed One, Jesus, born of the House of David, rules forever in the kingdom of God. He comes to reconcile all things in Himself, making peace through the Blood of His Cross. He alone is the alpha and omega of all that is. Praise to Jesus Christ, our King. Amen.

The Coming of the King

Lift up your gates, O princes. O eternal gates, let the King of glory enter. Thy throne, O God, is everlasting, for behold Thy King comes, the Savior of the world. In Him, we have remission of our sins and are made worthy partakers of His eternal love and life. He shall reign as King for ever and shall bless His people with peace. Amen.

St. Lawrence

LAWRENCE was born in Spain and became one of the seven deacons to serve Pope St. Sixtus II in Rome. He was entrusted with the care of the poor and the Church treasury. In the year 258 before his martyrdom, Pope Sixtus told Lawrence to sell the Church property and give the money to the poor. A Roman official heard of the exchange and insisted that Church property belonged to the Emperor. Lawrence presented to the official his beneficiaries, the poor people, who he said were the Church's wealth. The official was upset with Lawrence's embarrassing display of wealth and had Lawrence scourged, racked and fastened to a gridiron, where he was slowly roasted to death. During his suffering, Lawrence prayed for his persecutors and told them to turn him over, since he was sufficiently roasted on one side. Lawrence died a martyr for the sake of the poor. He is commemorated in the Canon of the Mass and is one of the most celebrated saints in the Church.

St. Lawrence, Martyr

O almighty God, we implore Thee to mercifully extinguish the flames of our vices even as You gave Your servant Lawrence the grace to overcome the fires of his torments and merit eternal salvation. We ask this through Christ our Lord. Amen.

Prayer to St. Lawrence

O glorious St. Lawrence, cheerful giver in the service of the poor, by your prayers, may we be purified by the cross of Christ that we may die to ourselves to bear the fruits of true justice. This we ask through our Lord Jesus Christ. Amen.

God's Deliverance

From the oppression of the flames of sin, I was not burnt.

The Little Flower

T HÉRÈSE OF THE CHILD JESUS AND THE HOLY FACE was canonized a saint on May 17, 1925 in St. Peter's Basilica by Pope Pius XI who also beatified her two years earlier. During the ceremony, roses that decorated the lights in the apse fell to the floor in an unknown way which was a sign that Thérèse was keeping her promise that "after my death I will let fall a shower of roses." Her roses were the little favors she granted to souls through her intercession, especially for missionaries and for the welfare of the Church. Thérèse began her consecrated life to God when she entered the Carmelite convent at Lisieux in 1888 to save souls and to pray for priests. She offered herself as a victim to God's merciful love so that souls would love God for all eternity. She believed in the "little way" of spiritual childhood, of humility and simplicity in all things in order to recognize her nothingness and her dependence on God. Thérèse made the love of God the mainspring of every action and accepted the crosses of life since "in this world there is no fruitfulness without suffering." In the cloistered garden of Carmel, she brought forth the flowers of Christian virtue, and the sweet fragrance of her roses drew others to the love of Jesus in Bethlehem, on Calvary and the Altar.

Prayer to St. Thérèse

Dear St. Thérèse, the Little Flower in God's heavenly garden, obtain from the Heart of Jesus, thy beloved Spouse, the favor I ask (*make your request*). Send me a rose of love that I will become more a child of God and serve the Church through my prayers that you may shower upon the Church roses of grace and virtue that God may be known and loved on earth and glorified forever in heaven. Amen.

St. Louis de Montfort

S T. LOUIS MARIE GRIGNION DE MONTFORT was born in 1673 in Montfort, France. He was educated by the Jesuits and ordained in 1700. He became a chaplain and then organized a group of women later known as the Daughters of Divine Wisdom. St. Louis was gifted with an irresistible prophetic eloquence. His preaching in the street, teaching of catechism and devotion to Mary brought many to his parish missions which consisted of the public recitation of the Rosary, renewal of baptism promises and candlelight processions. He effectively preached on the true devotion to Mary in which one becomes a slave of Jesus through Mary. For a time, he was forbidden to preach in France until Pope Clement XI approved of his missionary apostolate. He became a third order Dominican in 1710 and founded the Company of Mary in 1715. He died in 1716 and was canonized by Pope Pius XII in 1947. His book on *True Devotion to the Blessed Virgin Mary* is a spiritual battle plan for the defeat of the devil through a total consecration to Mary, the divine mould, who forms souls into the likeness of her Son, causing Jesus Christ to triumph.

St. Louis de Montfort

O Most loving Jesus, You have given me Your holy Mother to be my advocate before Your justice. By the prayers of St. Louis de Montfort, may I save my soul in union with Mary who will help me to do Your will and seek Your glory. In her motherly care, may she form Your likeness in my soul unto its fullness. Amen.

Prayer of St. Louis

I am all Thine and all I have is Thine, O most loving Jesus, through Mary, Thy holy Mother. Amen.

The Tree of Life

Happy is the soul in which Mary, the Tree of Life, is planted and which bears her fruit forever. Amen.

Blessed Margaret Castello

BLESSED MARGARET was born in 1287 in Meldola, Italy. She was blind, hunchback and lame and at the age of seven her parents had her imprisoned in a room, isolating her from society because her deformities were an embarrassment to them and dangerous to others. For several years, she was educated by a priest who visited her cell and brought her Holy Communion. She learned to love Jesus and accept her rejection in union with His sufferings. One day, her parents took Margaret to a Franciscan church in the city of Castello, hoping that she would be cured by the day's end. Because her condition remained the same, they abandoned her at the church. Margaret was rescued by families that cared for orphans and was taught how to beg for alms. Her love for God and innocence of life led her to become a third order Dominican. She dedicated her life to prayer and sacrifice, cured the lame and prophesied. During a visit to a prison in Castello, she attended to the prisoners and while praying for them, was raised in ecstasy off the floor to the astonishment of everyone present. Her love for God and neighbor knew no bounds. She died in 1320 and her cult was approved in 1609. She is the patroness of the unwanted, unplanned and unloved.

Blessed Margaret Castello

O God, Your love is everlasting and never leaves us orphans. Through the prayers of Blessed Margaret, may we despise all sin which deforms the soul and cherish the grace and innocence of life that reveals the dignity of the human person created and redeemed by Your Son. We ask this through Christ our Lord. Amen.

Loving His Will

O Lord, before I was, You knew me. You carved me in the palm of Your hand. I am grateful for Your gift of love and life which sustains me and I will meditate on Your commands which I love exceedingly. Your will is my peace and understanding. By Your grace I will glorify Your Name forever. Glory be to God. Amen.

St. Margaret Clitherow

MARGARET CLITHEROW was born at York, England in 1555. She married a wealthy butcher in 1571, raised three children and converted to the Catholic faith. Her husband was fined several times because she refused to support the Church of England and she was held for two years in a prison. Upon her release, Margaret established a Catholic school especially for children and provided a refuge in her home where priests could say Mass and find shelter from the persecutions against Catholics. She was placed under house arrest when she attempted to have her son educated in France. In 1586, she was found guilty of violating the law that prohibited the hiding of Catholic priests, when a search of her home revealed a secret hideout where Mass was said. Because she would not renounce her faith in the priesthood or her devotion to the Holy Sacrifice of the Mass, she was condemned to be crushed to death by an eight hundred pound weight. Margaret Clitherow was among the Forty Martyrs of England and Wales canonized by Pope Paul VI in 1970.

St. Margaret Clitherow

O God, by the love St. Margaret Clitherow had for the Holy Sacrifice of the Mass and the Catholic home, may parents realize their duty as the primary educators of their children to transmit the Catholic faith and make the sacramental life active in their home. We ask this through Christ our Lord. Amen.

Prayer for Priests

Lord Jesus, give Thy priests the grace to work for the sanctification of marriage and family life and the courage to instill in families the faith that teaches them to live for the kingdom of God. Who with the Father and the Holy Spirit lives and reigns in the undivided Trinity forever. Amen.

St. Mark

S T. MARK is one of the four evangelists, who, while in Rome, wrote the Second Gospel in Greek around the year 60 for the gentile converts. His gospel records the life of Jesus Christ according to the teachings of St. Peter, and reveals Jesus as the Divine Son of God. He came from a levitical family and his mother's home was a meeting place for the apostles in Jerusalem. He travelled with Paul and Barnabas, his cousin, on a mission journey to Antioch and Cyprus in the year 44. He met and worked with Sts. Peter and Paul in Rome, and became an interpreter and secretary to St. Peter, who called him "my son Mark." St. Paul said that "he is profitable to me for the ministry." Tradition credits him with establishing the Church in Alexandria, Egypt, where he was martyred in the year 74. He is the patron of Venice and of notaries, and his feast day is Apr. 25. He is symbolized by a lion because his gospel begins with the voice of John the Baptist "crying in the wilderness."

St. Mark, the Evangelist

O God, Who exalted blessed Mark, Thy Evangelist, by the grace of preaching the Gospel, grant, we beseech Thee, that we may ever profit by his teaching and be defended by his prayers. Through Jesus Christ our Lord. Amen.

The Greatest Commandment

Love God with all your heart.

Prayer of Faith

You are the Christ, Lord Jesus, the Son of God. May I not fear to lose my life for Your sake and the Gospel. Like You, may I be a servant to all, and accept little children in Your Name. May I not be ashamed to believe in Your Word that does not pass away, ready to meet You and the angels when You come in the glory of Your Father to judge the world. Amen.

Martha and Mary

MARTHA AND MARY lived in the village of Bethany, east of Jerusalem, where Jesus stayed at their home, was proclaimed "the Son of God" by Martha before raising Lazurus from the dead, and where Jesus was anointed with precious oil and began the journey for His triumphal entry into Jerusalem. On a visit to Martha and Mary, Jesus found Martha busy with "many things" while Mary, her sister, sat at His feet listening to His teaching. Martha asked Jesus to tell Mary to help her with the household tasks. But Jesus said that Mary had "chosen the better part" which shall not be taken from her. Jesus was teaching Martha that feeding the body is not as important as feeding the spiritual needs of the soul, and reminding her that "man does not live on bread alone, but on every word that comes from the mouth of God." Man was made to know, love and serve God and his work must be motivated by prayer which inspires deeds of charity. In the Eucharist, we must open the door of our heart to welcome Jesus into the home of clean heart where He will feed us with His Body and Blood and teach us to be the servants of His love.

Servants of Divine Love

God the Father of our Lord Jesus Christ, give us the grace to believe in the divinely revealed word of Your Son, that nourished by His Body and Blood, we may work and pray for Your glory as the servants of His divine love. We ask this through Christ our Lord. Amen.

Louis and Zélie Martin

LOUIS STANISLAUS MARTIN AND MARIE ZÉLIE GUÉRIN were married in Alençon, France on July 13, 1858. Both had previously desired to enter the religious life but were denied admission. Zélie asked God "to make me a mother of many children and to grant that all of them may be consecrated to Thee." Louis, a watchmaker, and his wife, Zélie, committed themselves to raise children for the glory of God and they dedicated each of their nine children to Mary Immaculate. Four of them died very young, while the others were destined for the convent. Louis called his youngest daughter, Marie Françoise Thérèse, his "little Queen." Louis and Zélie attended daily Mass together, observed the laws of the Church, practiced Christian virtue, prayed in common and cared for the poor. Zélie taught her children how to say their daily prayers. When she died, Louis moved his family to Lisieux. There he would take Thérèse on walks and fishing trips, read and sing to her at home and visit a Carmelite chapel. He encouraged Thérèse in her desire to become a Carmelite nun. At age fifteen, she was admitted to a Carmelite convent where four of her sisters had also entered. Louis gave thanks to God for "the honor He has done me in choosing His spouses from my household." Thérèse was very grateful to her parents for the blessings of a Catholic family life and in the convent she became "the Little Flower" to "offer our Lord the flowers of little sacrifices."

Sanctification of Family Life

O Lord Jesus Christ, Who was subject to Mary and Joseph and sanctified family life with grace and virtue, grant that we may learn from the Holy Family and attain eternal union with Thy family in heaven. Amen.

Peace in the Family

O Lord, through the intercession of Mary, the Mother of God, and blessed Joseph, we ask Thee to establish our families in Thy peace and grace that we may dwell in Thy home and praise Thee for ever and ever. Amen.

Mother Angelica

MOTHER ANGELICA, born Rita Rizzo in Canton, Ohio on Apr. 20, 1923, often suffered from her parents' divorce and from lack of food, adequate shelter and warmth. She graduated from Catholic grade school and helped her mother barely survive in a dry cleaning service. After a miraculous cure of a stomach ailment in 1943, she desired to be a bride of Jesus which led her on Aug. 15, 1944 to enter a Franciscan convent of Perpetual Adoration in Cleveland. She received the name Angelica and made her first profession in Canton in 1947. After recovering from a severe back injury, she fulfilled a promise made to God to build Him a new monastery and raised the funds for it by selling fishing lures. Permission was granted for a new foundation in Birmingham, Alabama where she became abbess of Our Lady of the Angels Monastery in 1962. Known for her perseverance, enthusiasm and blind faith, Mother Angelica entered the communications media to spread God's word and in 1981 founded EWTN, the first nationwide Catholic satellite television station. Through prayer and God's Providence, she has brought the love of Jesus and His truth into the homes of millions in booklets, television, tapes and short-wave radio. In the spirit of St. Francis, she has built up the Church and with childlike faith has been an instrument of God's miraculous grace.

God Alone

To receive You, dear Jesus, in Holy Communion is heaven on earth. I enter into Your Sacred Heart and You become first in my heart. May I attach myself to no one on earth but You alone, Who patiently waits for my undivided love. I belong to You before all others that I will become a child of the Father forever. Amen.

The Love of Jesus

May I love You, Jesus, more each day as I lovingly accept what You will for the good of my soul. I want to walk in Your footsteps and imitate Your love and life. I am confident that Your love is a love that does not fail and I trust in Your love to change the world. Your love, O Jesus, is the life of my soul. Amen.

Mother of Sorrows

OUR LADY, MOTHER OF SORROWS is a feast celebrated on Sept. 15 commemorating the seven sorrows or seven dolors of the Blessed Virgin Mary. The prophecy of Simeon, that her Son was a sign of contradiction destined for the fall and rising of many, was her first sorrow that culminated in the great sorrow of Calvary that pierced her own soul. At the foot of the cross, she was a light shining in the darkness of the human night, that retained belief in her Son's divinity. Like Abraham, she consented to the immolation of her Son, and for the salvation of the world, she suffered with her Son to bring forth God's spiritual children. In union with her sorrowful and Immaculate Heart, we must despise sin, and bear the crosses and trials of life with courage, patience and perseverance. Mary helps us to have true contrition and sorrow for sin, and to ask pardon for offenses committed against God's infinite goodness. The world can not fathom the offering of a Victim to satisfy the justice of God. But Mary, representing us on Calvary, offered prayers of faith and love for the sanctification and salvation of souls that her Son purchased by the shedding of His Precious Blood. She faithfully served the mystery of redemption that flows forth entirely from the merits of her Son, and we remember the indissoluble love of Jesus and Mary suffering for our salvation in the Holy Sacrifice of the Mass.

The Grace of Redemption

O God, at whose passion as Simeon had foretold, a sword of sorrow pierced the sweet soul of Mary, the glorious Virgin Mother, grant that we, who reverently recall her anguish and suffering, may obtain the blessed fruits of Thy redemption. Through Christ our Lord. Amen.

The Heart of Mary

O Most Sorrowful and Immaculate Heart of Mary,
pray for us, now and at the hour of our death. Amen.

Mother Teresa

MOTHER TERESA, Agnes Bojaxhiu, was born on Aug. 27, 1910 in Skopje, Albania. She was raised in a Catholic family and in 1928 joined the Loreto sisters in Ireland. She was sent to teach in India, where she taught for twenty years. On Sept. 10, 1946, she heard God calling her to follow Him in the slums and to serve Him in the poorest of the poor. She was given permission to leave the convent and to lead a religious life among the poor under obedience to the Archbishop of Calcutta. She began a school in the slums and cared for the sick. On Oct. 7, 1950, she founded the Missionaries of Charity to give wholehearted free service to the poor in homes for the dying, shelter for orphans, care for lepers, and feeding and clothing the destitute. Her sisters serve in all parts of the world working for the "salvation and sanctification of the poorest of the poor." The Holy Eucharist is the strength for their mission to be "God's love in action" serving Jesus in the "distressing disguise of the poor." In 1979, Mother Teresa received the Nobel Peace Prize for her worldwide mission to the poor. Her work of bringing Jesus to the poor in the spirit of Mary has inspired numerous vocations in her order, and has made her an incarnation of the beatitudes of Jesus to channel God's love in the modern world.

The Beatitudes

Blessed are the poor in spirit, for the kingdom of heaven is theirs. Blessed are they who mourn, for they shall be comforted. Blessed are the meek, for they shall inherit the earth. Blessed are they who hunger and thirst for holiness, for they shall be satisfied. Blessed are the merciful, for they shall receive mercy. Blessed are the pure of heart, for they shall see God. Blessed are the peacemakers, for they shall be called the children of God. Blessed are they who are persecuted for the sake of truth, for the kingdom of heaven is theirs.

"When I was hungry, you gave Me to eat"

St. Nicholas

NICHOLAS was born at Patara, a province of Lycia, and became the Archbishop of Myra in Asia Minor. He is reported to have been taken a prisoner during the persecution of Emperor Diocletian, and later to have attended the Council of Nicaea in 325 which firmly opposed the Arian heresy. He is known to have raised three children to life after they were pickled in a tub of salt water. He is believed to have saved three young women from prostitution when, on three separate occasions, he threw a bag of gold in the window of their home to provide them with a dowry for marriage. These miracles and incidents of charity are said to have started the tradition of St. Nicholas, or Santa Claus, who gives gifts and presents, especially to children, at Christmas. Santa Claus is a secular symbol of a bishop. His staff, cap, suit as well as his sleigh, gifts and elves are reminders of a bishop's crozier, mitre and priestly vestments, and that he rules as a spiritual king who dispenses the treasury of God's grace through the assistance of his priests. St. Nicholas died in 350 and is one of the most popular saints in all of Christendom. He is the patron saint of children, sailors and Russia.

St. Nicholas, Bishop

O God, Who granted to Thy holy Bishop Nicholas the grace of numerous miracles, may we through his merits and prayers be delivered from the everlasting flames of hell. Through Christ our Lord. Amen.

Prayer for Children

O St. Nicholas, protect our children from bodily and spiritual harm. May the birth of Jesus fill their hearts with love and joy, that they will follow your spirit of charity and grow in their love for God. Amen.

Merry Christmas!

St. Paul Miki and Companions

PAUL MIKI was born in 1564 at Tokushima, Japan. His family converted to Christianity when he was around the age of four. He entered a Jesuit seminary in 1584 and joined them in 1586. He was an excellent defender and preacher of the Christian faith, converting many non-believers to the faith. During a persecution in 1596, Paul and twenty-five other Catholics were sentenced to be crucified in Nagasaki. On Feb. 5, 1597, as they were led to the hill of crucifixion, they sang the *Te Deum*. While hanging on his cross, Paul preached a sermon inviting the bystanders to live and die for Christ. He forgave his executioner and then he and his companions were each lanced twice by a soldier. Paul Miki and his companions were among the 200,000 Christians that were the fruit of the missionary efforts of St. Francis Xavier who brought Christianity to Japan in 1549. Paul and his companions were canonized by Pope Pius IX on June 8, 1862.

St. Paul Miki, Martyr

Almighty God, grant that we may be strengthened in Thy love and delivered from all adversity through the merits of Thy martyr Paul Miki and his companions that we may rejoice in their fellowship in the everlasting bliss of heaven. Through Christ our Lord. Amen.

The Salvation of the Lord

The salvation of the just is from the Lord. He is their protection in time of trouble. Be not emulous of those who do evil, nor envy them that work iniquity. For the just cried out, and the Lord heard them and delivered them from all their troubles. God saves the humble of spirit. Amen.

APOSTLE of ROME

St. Philip Neri

ST. PHILIP NERI was born in Florence, Italy in 1515. He worked for his uncle until he decided to live in poverty in Rome and educate children. In 1544, after he experienced an ecstasy of God's love that enlarged his heart, he devoted himself to the study of theology and works of charity. In 1548, he founded a religious community that became the Congregation of the Oratory. He was ordained in 1551 and through the apostolic labors of his oratory, the fervor for Christian life was enlivened amidst the corruption in Rome. He promoted the frequent reception of the sacraments and the need for solid catechetical formation in the Catholic faith. He was known to raise the dead to life and because of his great love for the Eucharist, he would spend up to three hours offering the Holy Sacrifice of the Mass. Philip was an advisor to popes and cardinals and the spiritual charm of his cheerful, gentle character inspired in others a true love for God. He died in 1595 and was canonized in 1622. He is called the "Second Apostle of Rome."

St. Philip Neri

O Lord, Who inflamed the heart of Thy Confessor Philip with the fire of Thy love and made him zealous in the conversion of souls, grant that by his prayers we may love Thee faithfully and serve Thee with a gentle spirit. We ask this in the name of Jesus Christ our Lord. Amen.

Prayer to St. Philip

O gentle lover of God, St. Philip Neri, we ask that through our worthy reception of the sacraments and our fidelity to the teachings of Christ, we may increase our love for God and convert others by our example. We ask this through Jesus Christ our Lord. Amen.

St. Philomena

PHILOMENA, POWERFUL WITH GOD, is a title she earned through the miraculous favors of her powerful intercession. In 1802, a tomb containing the bones, skull and a vial of blood from a young girl was discovered in the catacombs of St. Priscilla in Rome. The tomb was marked with three red tiles on which was written "Peace be with you, Philomena" and on which there was etched a lily, anchor and arrows to indicate that she was a virgin-martyr. The relics were brought to a shrine in Mugnano, Italy in 1805 and thereafter visiting pilgrims received miraculous blessings and favors. In 1837, Pope Gregory XVI called Philomena "the wonder worker" and declared her a saint. He named her "Patroness of the Living Rosary." The Curé of Ars, who was devoted to St. Philomena, credited her with the many miraculous events in his village. Pope Pius IX made her "Patroness of the Children of Mary." St. Philomena was raised to the altar of sanctity solely through her powerful intercession, since details of her life were unknown. She is known to grant requests for conversions, cures, the resolution of marriage difficulties and is a powerful advocate before God for even the smallest favor.

Prayer to St. Philomena

O faithful and glorious virgin-martyr, St. Philomena, wonder worker of many miraculous favors. You know the needs of poor sinners. Graciously obtain from God the favor I now bring before you *(make your request)*. Through the merits of your suffering in union with the cross of Jesus, I believe you will answer my prayer. Amen.

Prayer for Faith

Dear St. Philomena, ever solicitous of the need for faith in God, by your powerful intercession, assist the Church in converting sinners, returning the fallen away to the practice of the Catholic faith, giving families the courage to follow the laws of God and helping priests to remain faithful in their vocations. We ask this through Christ our Lord. Amen.

The Poor Souls in Purgatory

T HE POOR SOULS IN PURGATORY are separated from the vision of God because they need to make satisfaction for the sins they committed during their lifetime on earth. They are suffering in fire worse than any earthly fire to expiate the temporal punishment due to their sins. The souls in purgatory are helpless and must rely on the prayers, good works and Masses offered on their behalf by the faithful in the Church on earth to relieve their suffering. It is a spiritual work of mercy and charity for the faithful on earth to pray for the poor souls, especially through the Holy Sacrifice of the Mass, which hastens their entrance into heaven. The poor souls are holy souls who will one day be perfectly purified to enter into the holy presence of God and who will not forget to pray for those who relieve their suffering. Through the worthy reception of the sacraments, penance, the patient bearing of suffering and the gaining of indulgences, the faithful can shorten or avoid time in purgatory. As members of the Body of Christ, the holy souls long for the glory of heaven that will unite them forever to the Bridegroom of their souls.

The Souls in Purgatory

O gentle Heart of Jesus, ever present in the Blessed Sacrament, ever consumed with burning love for the poor captive souls in purgatory, have mercy on them. Be not severe in Your judgments, but let some drops of Your Precious Blood fall upon the devouring flames. And, merciful Savior, send Your angels to conduct them to a place of refreshment, light and peace. Amen.

The Poor Souls

O Lord, the Creator and Redeemer of all the faithful, grant to the souls of Thy servants departed the remission of all their sins; that by the humble supplications of Thy Church, they may obtain the pardon which they have always desired of Thy Mercy. We ask this through Christ our Lord. Amen.

Lux aetérna lúceat eis

Pope John Paul II

POPE JOHN PAUL II, Karol Wojtyla, was born in Wadowice, Poland on May 18, 1920. Initially attracted to theatrical arts and poetry, he later studied in an underground seminary in Cracow and was ordained on Nov. 1, 1946. He received a doctorate in theology and was assigned to be an assistant pastor and chaplain. He became a professor of ethics and in 1958 was named an auxiliary bishop and in 1964 an archbishop. He attended Vatican Council II and contributed to *Gaudium et Spes*. In 1967, he was made a cardinal and served on the permanent council of the Bishop's Synod. Since his election to the Chair of Peter on Oct. 16, 1978, John Paul has travelled widely around the world bringing Christ's message of peace, reconciliation and truth. A prolific speaker and writer, he has proclaimed the transcendent dignity of the human person, upheld the teaching of *Humanae Vitae*, defended the irreplaceable role of the Christian family, reconfirmed Mary's exemplary presence in the life of the Church, and articulated the principles of morality. Under his reign, a Holy Year and Marian Year were celebrated, and a new code of canon law and a universal catechism were promulgated. He has courageously disciplined theologians and worked for an ecumenism that is faithful to Church doctrine. John Paul's apostolic mission is preparing the Church for a new evangelization to bring forth a culture of love and life and the glorification of God's holiness. On June 8, 1994 he said, "the man of the year 2000 must have Christ's Heart to know God and to know himself; he needs It to build the civilization of love."

Prayer to Mary

O Mary, Mother of Mercy, watch over all people, that the Cross of Christ may not be emptied of its power, that man may not stray from the path of the good or become blind to sin, but may put his hope ever more fully in God Who is "rich in mercy." May he carry out the good works prepared by God beforehand and so live completely "for the praise of His glory." Amen.

"The future of man passes by way of the family"

The Presentation of the Child Jesus

FORTY DAYS AFTER THE BIRTH OF JESUS, Mary and Joseph brought Him to the Temple in Jerusalem to consecrate Him to the Lord. They offered two turtledoves according to the law of Moses in gratitude for the deliverance of the Israelites in Egypt. The prophetess Anna and a holy and just man, the prophet Simeon, who prayed that before his death he would see the Messiah, were in the temple. Simeon recognized the Child in Mary's arms as the "anointed of the Lord." He took Him in his arms and proclaimed Him the Savior and Light of the nations, *"lumen ad revelatiónem géntium."* He prophesied that the Child was destined for the fall and rising of many in Israel, a sign of contradiction that would bring a sword of sorrow into Mary's Heart. Mary knew that Jesus was "the glorious King of the new Light," and she accepted God's will to bear the sorrow that would bring forth the salvation of souls. The feast of the Presentation, known as the Purification of Mary or Candlemas Day, is liturgically celebrated of Feb. 2 with a procession of lighted candles to signify that Jesus is the Light of the world. He entered the Temple of the Lord that we would find Him in the arms of Mary and offer ourselves to God with a pure heart.

The Presentation of the Lord

O Lord Jesus Christ, Who appeared among men in the substance of our flesh and was presented by Thy parents in the temple, and was recognized and received in the arms of the prophet Simeon and blessed by him, mercifully grant that, enlightened and taught by the grace of the Holy Spirit, we may truly acknowledge Thee and faithfully love Thee. Who with the Father and the Holy Spirit lives and reigns forever. Amen.

Queen of Heaven and Earth

MARY is Queen of heaven and earth and all creatures because she consented to be the Mother of the Incarnate Word. She became the Mother of the God-man, Who is the Lord and King of all things. From the moment of her Immaculate Conception, she surpassed all other creatures in the supernatural dignity of grace, virtue and glory which gave her the singular privilege of participating in her Son's work of salvation as His perfect disciple and collaborator. She shared in His victory over the dominion of Satan and sin and was assumed into heaven at the end of her life to become the Queen of His kingdom that has no end. Her royal rule is a superterrestial power of grace and love that leads souls to the kingdom of heaven. Mary exceeds all the angels and saints in the splendor of glory and is the highest creature in heaven next to the Blessed Trinity. As the first of the redeemed, she is a living and certain sign that those who follow her Son will receive the crown of everlasting life. Since the 4th century, the Church has honored Mary with the royal title of Queen and in 1954 Pope Pius XII established the feast of the Queenship of Mary.

Mary our Queen

We wish to exalt your Queenship and to recognize it as due to the sovereign excellence of your whole being, O dearest One, truly Mother of Him Who is King by right, by inheritance and by conquest. Reign, O Mother and Queen, by showing us the path of holiness and by guiding and assisting us that we may never stray from it. Amen.

The Queenship of Mary

Grant, we beg of You, O Lord, that we who honor the Blessed Virgin Mary, our Queen, may merit under her loving protection to attain peace on this earth and glory in heaven. Through Christ our Lord. Amen.

Queen of Mercy

Show us the kingdom of God.

St. Raphael and Tobias

RAPHAEL, an archangel who worships before the glory of God, was sent by God to cure the blindness of Tobit and give a husband to Sarah. Tobit was a just man who gave alms, fed the hungry, blessed God in all things and taught his son Tobias the ways of God. After burying a dead man one evening, Tobit was blinded by the droppings of sparrows. He became poor and told Tobias to go with a companion to recover his deposit of silver. Tobias found Raphael, known to him as Azarius. On the journey, Tobias caught a fish and Raphael told him to remove the heart, liver and gall for curative purposes. Raphael told Tobias about a kinswoman of his father, named Sarah. They visited Sarah's father and he agreed to the marriage even though she had seven husbands that were killed by a demon. On the wedding night, Tobias burned the heart and liver from the fish which drove away the demon and he and Sarah prayed for God's protection. When Sarah's father learned that God spared Tobias, he prepared a wedding feast. Raphael then recovered the silver and Tobias, Sarah and Raphael went to see Tobit who was overjoyed that they returned safely. After Tobias applied the gall to his father's eyes, Tobit could see again. Raphael refused any payment for his services and revealed to them his true identity. Tobit and his family then gave thanks to God, the King of the ages and Father forever.

St. Raphael

O God, Who gave St. Raphael the Archangel, the angelic physician of body and soul, to Thy humble servant Tobias as a companion on his journey, may he defend the sacrament of marriage from demonic powers and guide the faithful on the road to heaven where they will see Thy Face forever. Through Christ our Lord. Amen.

ST. RITA

wife

mother

Augustinian mystic

St. Rita of Cascia

ST. RITA was born near Spoletto, Italy in 1381. She desired to be a nun, but was married at the age of twelve in obedience to the plans of her parents. She became a faithful Catholic wife and mother and withstood the outrages and infidelities of her husband who eventually repented through her prayers. They were married eighteen years when he was killed. Her twin sons wanted to avenge their father's death, but Rita prayed they would not carry out their intention. A short time later, they died of an illness after receiving the Last Sacraments. As a widow, Rita attempted to enter the religious life several times, and in 1413 was finally admitted into an Augustinian convent at Cascia. She desired to participate in the sufferings of Christ and, in a mystical experience in 1441, she received a permanent wound from a thorn on a crucifix which caused her much suffering the rest of her life. She died in 1457 and her body has remained incorrupt. Many miracles have occurred at her tomb and her intercession has brought many back to the Church. She was canonized in 1900 and is a patroness of impossible cases.

St. Rita of Cascia

O God, Who gave to St. Rita the grace to partake of Thy Passion and to bear on her forehead a sacred wound from Thy crown of thorns, grant that, by her merits and prayers, we may learn to love our enemies and to have true contrition and sorrow for our sins. We ask this through Christ our Lord. Amen.

Prayer to St. Rita

O St. Rita, by your love of neighbor and devotion to the Passion of Jesus which purified your soul, obtain for me the grace to imitate your example of penance, perseverance and trust in Divine Providence that will convert sinners and defeat the spirit of enmity. We ask this through Jesus Christ our Lord. Amen.

Archbishop Fulton J. Sheen

FULTON J. SHEEN was born May 8, 1895 in El Paso, Illinois to Newton Sheen and Delia (Fulton) Sheen. He was baptized Peter, but later took his mother's maiden name. His father ran a hardware store and owned farm lands, where his sons milked cows, fed pigs and made hay. The family rosary was said every evening and priests visited their home frequently. He attended Catholic grade school in Peoria, was high school salutatorian and after college enrolled at the St. Paul Seminary in St. Paul, Minnesota. Ordained on Sept. 20, 1919, he went on to receive advanced degrees from Louvain and Rome. After a year of parish work, he joined the philosophy faculty at the Catholic University of America. In 1950, he became a national missions director and in 1951 was consecrated a bishop in Rome. He attended Vatican Council II and in 1966 was appointed bishop of Rochester, New York and named a titular Archbishop in 1969. An exceptionally gifted speaker and media apostle of God's word, who began each day with a Holy Hour, Archbishop Sheen reached millions in his more than twenty-five years of radio and television broadcasting. His numerous books, tapes, retreats and sermons inspired a Catholic fervor and won many converts. His deep love for God and the Church helped others to find the faith in Christ that made life worth living. He died in 1979.

For the Propagation of the Faith

O God, Who wills that all men may be saved and come to the knowledge of Thy Truth, we beg Thee to send forth many laborers into Thy harvest, that with the help of Thy grace they may boldly proclaim Thy word and glorify Thy Name before the nations so that all men may know Thee and Thy Son, Jesus Christ, Whom Thou has sent for the salvation of their souls. Amen.

St. Stephen

STEPHEN, meaning "crown," was a convert to Christianity in the first century and was ordained a deacon by the Apostles to care for the poor in Jerusalem. He was an excellent preacher, alive with the Holy Spirit in his defense of God's truth. Renowned for his virtue, he worked great miracles and signs and converted many to the Christian faith. He was accused of speaking contrary to the authority of God and Moses and had to defend himself before the officials in Jerusalem. His face looked like that of an angel when he spoke of Jesus, Whom he saw in the heavens at the right hand of God. The eloquent wisdom and testimony of his faith in Jesus angered his accusers and they dragged him outside the city where they stoned him to death. As he was dying, he prayed for the forgiveness of his executioners and said, "Lord Jesus, receive my spirit...Lord, lay not this sin to their charge." St. Stephen was the first martyr of the Church and is commemorated in the Canon of the Mass.

St. Stephen

O God, grant that we may learn to love our enemies as we celebrate the heavenly birthday of Thy holy servant Stephen who prayed for his persecutors to the Lord Jesus, Thy Son, Who lives and reigns with Thee in the unity of the Holy Spirit for ever and ever. Amen.

Words of St. Stephen

Moses performed wonders and signs in Egypt. Behold I see the heavens opened and Jesus standing at the right hand of the power of God. Lord Jesus, receive my spirit and lay not this sin to their charge.

"Blessed are they who follow the law of the Lord"

St. Teresa of Ávila

S T. TERESA OF JESUS was born on Mar. 28, 1515 in Ávila, Spain. At an early age she enjoyed reading the lives of the saints, and was devoted to Sts. Augustine and Mary Magdalen, and to St. Joseph who cured her of a crippling disease. After her mother died, she was educated at a convent, and then eventually decided in 1534 to enter the Carmelite convent of the Incarnation in Ávila. In 1562 she became the foundress of a convent dedicated to St. Joseph, and began a reform in the Carmelite order for more detachment, penance, silence and prayer. She founded sixteen convents, and with the help of St. John of the Cross, she formed the Discalced Carmelites. Her reform was recognized by Pope Gregory XIII. St. Teresa combined mystical contemplation with great practical accomplishments. She was a mystic who wrote several famous books about her union with God, and was an exceptional teacher of prayer, gifted with wise judgement and the grace of mystical marriage. She died on Oct. 4, 1582 and was canonized in 1622. St. Teresa was declared a Doctor of the Church by Pope Paul VI on Sept. 27, 1970. She is usually pictured with an angel piercing her heart.

St. Teresa, Virgin

Graciously hear us, O God our Savior, that as we rejoice in the glory of Thy Virgin, Teresa, so we may be fed with the food of her heavenly teaching, and grow in loving devotion for Thee. We ask this through Christ our Lord. Amen.

St. Teresa's Bookmark

Let nothing disturb you; nothing frighten you. All things are passing. God never changes. Patience obtains all things. Nothing is wanting to him who possesses God. God alone suffices.

The Glory of Truth

May God who favors truth be praised! May it please His Majesty
that this all be for His honor and glory.

Blessed Teresa Benedicta

BLESSED SISTER TERESA BENEDICTA OF THE CROSS, known as Edith Stein, was born on Oct. 12, 1891 in a devout Jewish family at Breslau, Silesia. As a youth, she lost her faith in God and in her search for truth, she studied phenomenology and became a philosopher. After reading the autobiography of St. Teresa of Ávila, she decided to become a Catholic and was baptized on Jan. 1, 1922. Her conversion was an intellectual and spiritual union that recognized God as the essential foundation for all existence. She taught for eight years at a Dominican convent school and on Oct. 14, 1933 entered the Discalced Carmelite convent in Cologne, and then took the name Teresa Benedicta of the Cross. She desired to suffer with Christ in His redemptive work to "offer myself to the Heart of Jesus as sacrificial expiation for the sake of the world." During the Nazi persecution in Germany in 1938, she moved to the Carmel of Echt, Holland. In 1942, she and her sister were among the Catholics of Jewish descent that were arrested by the Nazis and sent to Auschwitz where they died in the gas chambers on Aug. 9, 1942. Her heroic love for Christ and the Jewish people led her to participate in the Passion of Christ that unites the soul to Truth itself. She was beatified on May 1, 1987.

The Truth of the Cross

Lord Jesus, on the Cross You are the power of God and the wisdom of God. Your Blood is the curtain by which we enter the Holiest of Holies and are cleansed of our sins, our eyes are opened to Your eternal light and our ears hear Your divine truth. Through the prayers of Blessed Teresa Benedicta, may we be nourished by Your Body and Blood and become one with Your Flesh and Blood that we may offer ourselves to Your holy will. Amen.

St. Thomas Aquinas

S T. THOMAS AQUINAS, the Angelic Doctor, was born near Aquino, Italy in 1225. At age five, he was educated at Monte Cassino. In 1243, he joined the Dominicans, but his family disagreed, holding him captive for two years. But he prevailed, and rejoined the order in 1245. He studied under St. Albert the Great, overcame the name "dumb ox," and became his assistant. He was ordained and then became a master of theology, frequently lecturing in Paris and Rome. He was adept in refuting error and defending Catholic truth. His eloquence and precise exposition demonstrated the intellectual coherence of Divine Revelation. He achieved a synthesis between faith and reason and wrote many scholarly works, among them the *Summa Theologiae*, his monumental masterpiece. He was an outstanding preacher, teacher and intellectual genius whose theological work was founded upon his love for the immutable truths revealed by God. Numerous pontiffs recognized the essence of his thought, and it became official Church teaching. He was a man of great humility who wrote excellent hymns and prayers. He died on Mar. 7, 1274 on his way to the Second Council of Lyons. He was canonized in 1323 and declared a Doctor of the Church in 1567. Pope Leo XIII made him patron of Catholic schools. He once said, "the Church of Peter flourishes in faith and is immune from error." St. Thomas was a theological sun that nourished the world with the brilliance of Divine Truth.

St. Thomas, Doctor

O God, Who gave glory to the Church with the inspired teaching of St. Thomas, Your holy Confessor, and rendered it fruitful by his holy deeds, grant that we may understand what he taught and follow his good example. Through Christ our Lord. Amen.

O Sacrum Convivium

O Sacred Banquet wherein Christ is received; the memory of His Passion is renewed, the mind is filled with grace, and the pledge of future glory is given unto us. Amen.

Tu Rex Gloriae, Christe.

"I am willing to accept any child.."

"who would be aborted and to give that
child to a married couple who will love
the child and be loved by the child."
Mother Teresa of Calcutta

The Unborn Child

MOTHER TERESA OF CALCUTTA, INDIA, foundress of the Missionaries of Charity, spoke to the National Prayer Breakfast attended by representatives from over one hundred nations in Washington, D.C. on Feb. 3, 1994. In her address, she said, "the greatest destroyer of peace today is abortion because it is a war against the child, a direct killing of the innocent child." "By Abortion, the mother does not learn to love, but kills her own child to solve her problems." The "unborn child has been carved in the hand of God from conception and is called by God to love and to be loved, not only now in this life, but forever." When "living love is destroyed by contraception, abortion easily follows...which brings a people to be spiritually poor." "*I am willing to accept any child who would be aborted*" and "I will never give a child to a couple who have done something not to have a child." "Any country that accepts abortion is not teaching its people to love, but to use violence to get what they want." By loving others "America can become...a sign of care for the weakest of the weak, the unborn child." Through the patronage of St. Joseph and Our Lady of Guadalupe, the mission and destiny of the child revealed in the Child Jesus is realized in the prophetic voice of Mother Teresa that "the child is God's gift to the family."

Prayer for the Unborn Child

Heavenly Father, Creator of human life, watch over the unborn child that You made in Your image and likeness. Help all families to welcome Your gift of the child who is destined for the glory of eternal life. May the nations of the world protect Your precious gift of unborn human life from its very beginning, and safeguard the Christian family through which true peace is found in society. Amen.

"Love begins at home in the family"

St. Vincent de Paul

V INCENT DE PAUL was born on Apr. 24, 1580 in Pouy, France. He was a gifted student and was ordained in 1600 at age twenty. He was captured by pirates during a sea voyage and sold into slavery in Algeria. He was freed after he converted one of his slave masters. He studied in Rome and later did parish missions in France. He became a follower of St. Francis de Sales and then ministered to the destitute and the poor. He founded the Congregation of the Mission and the Sisters of Charity, dedicated to alleviating human suffering and poverty. St. Vincent also established hospitals, orphanages and sheltered victims of war and provided refuge for Christian slaves. He opened a seminary and did spiritual writing. He was known for his deeds of charity through his relief organizations that were open to all classes of people. He was a spiritual father of orphans and lived "to plant the Gospel-spirit of charity, humility, meekness and simplicity in the hearts of all Christians." He died on Sept. 27, 1660 and was canonized in 1737. He is the patron of charitable societies and his work continues in organizations such as the St. Vincent de Paul Society.

Prayer to St. Vincent de Paul

O glorious St. Vincent, heavenly patron of charitable societies and spiritual father of those in misery, while on earth you extended a kindly hand to the needy. Through your merciful intercession, obtain help for the destitute, relief for the abandoned, solace for the unfortunate, comfort for the sick and the grace of preaching the Gospel to the poor. May your example of charity encourage priests to work for the salvation of all souls that the love of Christ may be known to all people. We ask this through Christ our Lord. Amen.